Copyright © 2016 by Lani Sharp
All rights reserved. This book or any portion thereof
may not be reproduced or used in any manner whatsoever
without the express written permission of the publisher
except for the use of brief quotations in a book review.

Printed in Australia

First Printing, 2016

ISBN 978-0-9945051-2-5

White Light Publishing House
6 Lincoln Way
Melton West, VIC, Australia 3337

www.whitelightpublishingau.com

❧ DEDICATION ☙

This book is dedicated to my soul sister Jo-Anne, a bright-shining, generous, special, spirited lioness who I have only known since I lived in Darwin (two years ago at the time of writing). JoJo, our Darwin connection will always bind us together. I have special memories of your visits, however fleeting. We both know that the essence of a connection is not the length of time you've known someone, but rather the impact that they've made.

This book is also dedicated to my true soul friend, who supports everything I do, understands me, complements me and shares my spiritual visions and aspirations. I love you eternally and unconditionally. Your big heart, loyalty, generosity, love, affection, and sense of fun, warmth, strength, courage, adventure, wanderlust, and luminosity shine bright and eternal. I love you without beginning and without end, for you were always there, the best part of my All That Is. Thank you for entering my life when I needed you most. You know who you are, for I, too, have always been in you.

ABOUT THE AUTHOR

☾ ★ ☽

Lani Sharp is a Natural Born Rebel who just also happens to be an Aquarian, who shunned 'conventional' astrology courses to pursue her own path in the wondrous, inspiring and ever-evolving field of cosmic forces and stellar influences. After failing to find a course or tutor that suited her needs, Lani set out on her own starry Magic Carpet adventure across the skies, partly to discover her own 'truths' about this ancient system, but mostly to prove that one can achieve absolutely anything, including and above all, their dream careers (or lifestyle), if they put their hearts and souls into it. A self-taught astrologer who takes the esoteric and spiritual approach to this much-loved popular art, she has been studying and effectively practising astrology since she was eight years old. When she is not writing about, channelling, practising or teaching astrology, she can be found living her dream life alternating somewhere between her home in Australia's stunning Tropical North or her second home in Victoria's beautiful Dandenong Ranges, enjoying tea parties with her highly imaginative Cancerian daughter, Allira, and their gnome and fairy friends, crystal-wishing, day-dreaming, believing in gnomes, pixies, angels, fairies, magic and miracles, honing her magickal * witchcraft skills, Moon-gazing, Sun-worshipping, Venus-channelling, Jupiter-drawing, assisting others to discover, unravel and follow their true spiritual paths … or of course walking across rainbows!

Not a mistake. Magick is a Wiccan variation of the word 'magic'.

★

ACKNOWLEDGEMENTS, CREDITS & GRATITUDE BLESSINGS

☆

I would love to thank the following people and entities for their amazing contributions, interest, support and faith in me as I wrote the manuscripts for each of the twelve astrological Sun signs. Firstly, the biggest thank you go to my Mum, Sandra, and my stepdad, Barry, for their unending support, love, advice, daily Skype conversations, acceptance of our geographical distance, and above all, their inner knowing that everything always comes together in the end. Your support of me and my dreams is appreciated beyond words. Secondly, gratitude to my wonderful partner, Travis, for his patience (no mean feat for a Gemini!), for supporting me every step of the way, and for his acceptance of my 'mad scientist' Aquarian mindset by never trying to break down the invisible 'laboratory' walls I built around myself while writing the books. I would also like to extend my enormous gratitude to the following: Allira, my little Cancerian 'crab' daughter, a soul in a billion, who also had to tolerate and operate within the bounds of her nutty professor mother's antics and focus throughout the writing of the books. Thank you to Nicola, my wonderful Facebook friend, for recommending White Light Publishing House, and of course to White Light Publishing House themselves, for pouring their faith and passion into my project from the very beginning - and an even bigger thank you to the wonderful people behind the company for publishing my work, Christie and Jess! Gratitude also goes out to my dear friends, both near and far, who have inspired in me so many ideas through simply being themselves - especially Amanda and Carlie. Amanda, you have always been my 'astrology buddy' and I have always enjoyed - and learned so much through - our discussions on all things astrology and star signs: the good, the bad and the ugly! Having someone like you off which to bounce thoughts and share ideas with, has always been immensely helpful and appreciated. I have saved my final thank you for The Universe, who always delivers to me exactly what I have asked for, without exception. The Universe is my ultimate *higher power*, my guiding light, my powerful driving force, my spiritual helper, my guardian angel, my eternal friend, my inner motivator, my sympathetic listener, my inspirational teacher, and the fulfiller of all my dreams, including this one, having my very first book(s) published, a long-held dream that stretches way back through the years to my days of being a mini dreamer, inquisitor and stargazer. The Universe has always believed in me, but perhaps more importantly, I have always believed in *IT*.

So to all of the above, I wish to say:

Thank you, thank you, thank you!

"There was a star danced,
and under that I was born"

William Shakespeare

"We were born at a given moment, in a given place, and like vintage years of wine, we have the qualities of the year and of the season in which we are born"

Carl G. Jung

INSPIRED BY ALL THE SIGNS

Aries imparted courage and boldness
And helped me dance away the pain
Taurus gave me hugs and comfort
And shelter from the rain
Gemini provided me with laughter
And taught me again how to have fun
Cancer nurtured and sustained me
By reflecting back my Sun
Leo reminded me there was joy
From within myself and above
Virgo awakened my healthy glow
By teaching me how to love
Libra gave me gentle hugs
And judged me not for a thing
Scorpio lent me some of his power
And took away the sting
Sagittarius showered me with gifts
Of words so wise and true
As Capricorn led the way up the mountain
My resolve and strength grew
Aquarius gave me the gift of friendship
And carried me as his brother
And Pisces swam with me to the depths
With a compassion like no other.

Special Note

Throughout the text of this book, and indeed the whole Lucky Astrology book series, I have capitalised the first letter of the word 'Universe'. This is because, quite simply, I feel it is a very special title for the higher power that I personally choose to be guided by, and have accordingly highlighted it as such.

You may also notice that I use the words 'he' or 'she', and 'his' or 'her', when referring to your own Sun sign and other zodiac signs, and never 'he or she' or 'his or her' together. The reason for this is for simplicity, for I don't wish the sentences to be too wordy and therefore the messages within them to be lost. As a general rule, I refer to all six 'masculine' zodiac signs as 'he', and all six 'feminine' signs as 'she', and this remains a consistent rule throughout this book and the whole series.

Your Sun sign, Leo, is a masculine sign and will thus be referred to accordingly.

CONTENTS

	Page
ASTROLOGY	15
THE ZODIAC & YOUR PLACE IN THE SUN	24
LEO THE LION	31
QUOTES BY LEONINES	37
THE LEO CONSTELLATION	42
THE LEO SYMBOL	45
THE RUNDOWN & LESSONS ★	
THE ESSENCE OF LEO	48
THE THREE DECANS OF LEO	58
YOUR ELEMENT ★ FIRE	62
YOUR MODE ★ FIXED	84
YOUR RULING PLANET ★ THE SUN	87
YOUR HOUSE IN THE HOROSCOPE ★	
THE FIFTH HOUSE	100
YOUR OPPOSITE SIGN ★ AQUARIUS	104
MAGIC, DRAWING, ATTRACTION, SPELLS,	
RITUALS, WISHING & POWER	113
ASTROLOGY & MAGIC	118
PLANETS ★ DAYS OF THE WEEK	
& THEIR POWERS	124
YOUR NATAL MOON PHASE	128
SPELLS, MAGIC & WISHING WITH MOON PHASES	131
THE MOON ★ WHAT T REPRESENTS IN THE	
HUMAN PSYCHE & NATAL CHART	138
YOUR MOON SIGN	141
YOUR BODY & HEALTH	149
THE CELL SALTS ★ ASTROLOGICAL TONICS	155

	Page
FIRE SIGN LEO & THE CHOLERIC HUMOUR	158
MONEY ATTRIBUTES	161
COLOURS ★ YOUR LUCKY COLOURS	164
LUCKY CAREER TIPS	176
LUCKY PLACES	181
GEMS & CRYSTALS	182
LEONINE POWER CRYSTALS	195
YOUR LUCKY NUMBERS	204
YOUR LUCKY MAGIC HOURS OR TIME UNITS	212
YOUR LUCKY DAY ★ SUNDAY	217
YOUR LUCKY CHARM / TALISMANS	221
YOUR LUCKY ANIMALS & BIRDS	224
YOUR METALS	237
PLANTS, HERBS, SPICES, TREES, SHRUBS, FLOWERS, SCENTS & INCENSE	242
YOUR FOODS	248
YOUR LUCKY WOOD & CELTIC TREE ★ WALNUT & HOLLY OR HAZEL	250
THE POWER OF LOVE	256
LUCKY IN LOVE? LEO COMPATIBILITY	268
YOUR TAROT CARDS	285
LUCKY 13 TIPS	304
HAVE YOU PACKED YOUR MAGICAL BAG FOR THE JOURNEY?	307
A FINAL WORD ★ TAPPING INTO THE MAGIC OF LEO	308

LUCKY ASTROLOGY

By Lani Sharp

*Tapping into the Powers of Your Sun Sign for Greater
Luck, Happiness, Health, Abundance & Love*

"That which is above is like to that which is below, and that which is below is like to that which is above, to accomplish the miracles of one thing … the Father thereof is the Sun, the mother the Moon."

The Emerald Tablet, Hermes Trismegistus, (circa 3000 BC)

★ ASTROLOGY ★

Astrology: "Divination through the correlation of
earthly events with celestial patterns"
'Real Magic', I. Bonewits, 1971

A BRIEF HISTORY

Astrology can be defined as the calculation and meaningful interpretation of the positions and motions of the heavenly bodies, and their correlation with human experiences. Its central concept is based upon this interconnectedness or correspondence between the stars and ourselves.

The word astrology is derived from the Greek word astron, meaning 'star' and logos which means 'word'. Astrology, therefore, literally means language of the stars. It is based on the ancient law known as 'As Above, So Below', otherwise known as the Law of the Macrocosm and Microcosm. The Macrocosm is the Universe, symbolised by the sky, the starry dome that we can see from the Earth; the Microcosm is us - humans, and all other life on Earth. 'As Above, So Below' is a well-known and deeply impressing maxim of Hermetic origin, inscribed upon the famed Emerald Tablet among cryptic wording by enigmatic figure, Hermes Trismegistus, around 5,000 years ago. These four powerful words are adopted by astrologers and believers in magic to explain, in very succinct wording, the meaning behind the art and science of celestial influences upon our Earthly affairs.

Astrology and many other magical and occult studies, propose that we are not separate from the Universe, we are part of it. The Sun, Moon and planets all follow exact patterns of movement and their motions can be measured precisely by astronomers. The basic idea of astrology is that all individual parts of the Universe, from plants to animals, cooperate with each other and work together in harmony.

Anyone can apply astrological knowledge in their daily lives, but it hasn't always been like that. At one time, astrology was reserved only for Kings and nations, and only the court astrologer/astronomer could cast and interpret horoscopes. Ancient astrology and astronomy used to be one and the same. To be an astrologer, you first had to be able to interpret the stars in some systematic way, and then track the movement of the Moon and the planets against the background of the constellations.

Astrology, the knowledge and language of the cosmos, goes back to the ancient kingdom of Babylonia and was adapted by the Mesopotamians, Greeks, Egyptians and Romans to incorporate their own deities (as indicated in mythology). It is upon a combination of Greek and Egyptian interpretations of astrology that our present knowledge is based.

In the ancient Mesopotamian world, as far back as 800 BC, people lived precariously beneath the open skies. The skies and the stars which filled them, were the real founders of astrology. Today we are aware that the Sun and Moon exert a profound influence upon our Earthly affairs, but for our primitive ancestors, the heavens, the stars and the planets must have been a matter of great and mysterious significance. Early humankind, its senses influenced by natural processes of ebbs, flows, growth, decay and cycles, tended naturally towards a physical explanation of the Universe. At first, the movements of the planets - and all celestial occurrences - were observed as omens affecting the Ruler and his nation; it was only in Egypt in the fifth century AD that the casting of horoscopes for individual people and the calculation of the planetary positions at the time of birth became widespread.

The first astrologers, the Chaldeans, mapped the stars and later passed this knowledge and wisdom on to the ancient Greeks, who, during the third century BC, developed astrology into a science with the use of mathematical aids and instruments to measure planetary movements. The Greeks were the first to cast individual horoscopes. And it was the Greeks who associated the four elements with the signs of the zodiac. The word "zodiac" can be translated from Greek to mean the "circle or path of the animals." The Greeks not only had names for the twelve Solar phases but had symbols for each, and many correspond with the ones we use today.

The Greeks passed on much of their knowledge to the Romans. During the second century BC, Roman astrologers were primarily forecasters who were consulted frequently by rulers of the church and state. By the early third century AD, astrology co-existed with early Christianity. This harmonious co-existence was possible because it was considered that celestial bodies could foretell events, but did not determine the future - indeed, the stars seen by the shepherds at the time of Christ's birth were only predictors of his arrival. After the fourth century AD, Christianity strengthened and the popularity of astrology declined as Christian reluctance to support 'pagan' or 'superstitious' beliefs became more prominent. The Middle Ages saw a revival in astrology, with courses being taught in universities and other educational establishments, and connections were made between the zodiac, alchemy, herbs and medicine. Astrology was once again able to exist alongside the Church, although many remained suspicious of astrologers.

Around the beginning of the fifteenth century, academics of the Renaissance movement examined the past for knowledge, and ancient philosophies, including astrology, flourished; this coincided with arts and science movements developing. The famous prophet and astrologer Nostradamus lived during this period. Leonardo da Vinci depicted aspects of astrology combined with geometry in his art. Writers and poets of the time, including Shakespeare, alluded to zodiacal influences in their work.

During this period, astrology had numerous practical applications. Agricultural calendars were introduced, indicating favourable planting times according to the phases of the Moon; health and illness were linked with movements of celestial bodies; and emotional states and mental health afflictions correlated with the planetary positions.

Eventually, new ways of thinking led to a split between astronomy and astrology, and by the seventeenth century, the realm of science had developed to such a degree that astrology was no longer taken seriously.

The study of the sky above us has been charted for more than 5,000 years. This fact is known because ancient 'horoscopes' imprinted on clay tablets have been unearthed, dating back almost 5,400 years ago. However, no one knows for certain just how, when and where astrology first began, although it is known that it flourished in ancient Chaldea, Mesopotamia, Babylon and Egypt.

Astrology is a science which has spanned many centuries and still remains extraordinarily popular, and its truths have the potential to speak to and through *through* all of us. Long before today's interest in it, men of great vision such as Ptolemy, Hippocrates, Plato, Galileo, Jefferson, Franklin, Newton, Columbus and Jung respected its inherent truths, mythology and eternal knowledge. Furthermore, astrology predates many other 'sciences' - for out of it grew religion, medicine and astronomy, not the other way around.

The discipline of astrology is ultimately a study of the interlocking and interrelated forces of the twelve zodiacal forces, or constellations, that grace the heavens, as they pour their energies into the Earthly kingdoms below. As these various energies circulate throughout the etheric realm of our Solar system, these zodiacal entities and archetypes imprint their vibrational frequencies and harmonic resonances upon our bodies, minds, souls and spirits.

ASTROLOGY & THE INDIVIDUAL

Since the earliest period of the history of humankind, people studied the starry vaults of the heavens and conceived that their presence, movements and positions endowed planet Earth's inhabitants with Divine influence. There is much evidence that positions and movements of the planets as seen from Earth at the time of a birth are linked to personality characteristics of individuals. Human energy and emotional cycles are governed by the forces and networks of magnetic impulses from all the planets. Of all the heavenly bodies, the Moon's effects and power are the most marked and visible due to its close proximity to Earth. But the Sun, Venus, Mars, Mercury, Jupiter, Saturn, Uranus, Neptune and Pluto exercise their influences just as surely. In fact, scientists are aware that plants and animals are affected by natural cycles which are governed by forces such as fluctuations in barometric pressure, the gravitational field and electricity in the air. These Earthly dynamics are originally triggered by magnetic vibrations from the atmosphere, or outer space, from where the planets send forth their unseen waves. No living organism or mineral on Earth escapes these immense, if unseen, influences.

The geomagnetic field seems to affect life on Earth in certain observed ways, and these influences appear to correlate with planetary positions. It has been suggested that the fluctuations of the Earth's magnetic field are picked up by the nervous system of the in utero infant, which acts like an antenna, and these synchronise the internal biological clocks of the foetus which control the moment of birth. The foetal magnetic antenna therefore, is sensitive enough to sense these planetary vibrations and fields, and through a combination of inherited genetics and the positions of the planets at birth, they are imprinted with certain basic inherited and 'absorbed' personality characteristics.

Carl Jung, the Swiss psychiatrist and psychological theorist, suggested that the inherent disposition of the individual is present at birth, and is reflected in the patterns of his or her natal chart. Further, he theorised that there is a 'priori factor' in all human activities, namely the inborn, preconscious and unconscious individual structure of the psyche. The preconscious psyche, for example that of a newborn baby, is not simply an empty vessel into which practically anything can be poured, but rather it is this preconscious psyche that gives us the free will to become what we are instead of what others or our environment makes us. The child is not merely a receptacle for the psychic life of those around him or her, albeit sensitive and susceptible to the surrounding unconscious forces in childhood; for he/she also brings something of his own to his experience of them.

Further, Dr Harold S. Burr, who was a Professor of Anatomy at the Yale University School of Medicine, and author of *The Nature of Man and the Meaning of Existence* (1962), asserted that there is order in the Universe, unity in the organism and man is endowed with a soul. He stated that a complex magnetic field not only establishes the pattern of the human brain at birth, but continues to regulate and control it through life, and that the human central nervous system is a superb receptor of electro-magnetic energies, indeed the finest in nature. He contended that the electro-dynamic fields of all living things, which may be measured and mapped with standard voltmeters, mould and control each organism's development, health and mood, and named these fields 'fields of life'.

It can therefore be suggested that astrological and planetary influences endow us with the majority of our characteristics at birth, characteristics bestowed upon us according to our Sun sign and other planetary forces. Other parts of the chart are also highly significant and need to be integrated for a 'whole' picture to form, however the Sun sign is an excellent starting point.

The ancients taught that astrology was one of the keys to the many enigmas that plague humans in their unceasing quest to determine what the meaning of life is, and what their role and place in the Universe is - and this quest still persists today. Astrology, which dates back over 5,000 years, is indeed one such key to unlocking the many secrets of the Universe - and ultimately, the individual self.

"KNOW THYSELF"

"Man, know thyself. All wisdom centres on this."
Carl Jung

Before the temple of the Oracle at Delphi, the ancient Greeks imparted a special piece of advice that was carved onto one of the portals: "Know Thyself." These two powerful words are easy enough to understand, but much more difficult to apply. Throughout life's inner and outer journey, astrology can provide us with an inner navigational system by which we can be guided towards our highest potential, and closer towards the eternal quest of 'knowing thyself'. It provides the hope that this higher spiritual plane exists and that if we can 'read' and therefore be guided by the unique inner blueprint that our individual birth chart has stamped upon us at the moment we take our very first breath, indeed we can reach this higher spiritual plane and realise our innate potential.

Always remember that astrology is not fatalistic. The stars may incline, but they do not compel. Astrology simply provides us with an inner guide, a blueprint, for our journey through life and the finding of our true selves - and what we do with the resulting knowledge is entirely up to us.

Good luck on your journey!

THE ZODIAC & YOUR PLACE IN THE SUN

The zodiac is a circle of 360 degrees, consisting of equal segments of 30 degrees each. These represent the twelve houses of the twelve astrological signs. This zodiac is how the early astrologers imagined the Solar system to be, a perfect circle with the Earth at its centre, around which the Sun, Moon and the planets revolved. Each sign of the zodiac corresponds to one of the twelve segments, following a chronological order and established according to the rhythm of the seasons and cycles of the Sun and the Moon. But the zodiac itself, or the band of constellations which comprise it, has shifted over the millennia, creating division between astronomical and astrological schools of thought. It has been said that due to this shift over time, one who once considered themselves as an Aquarian, is actually a Capricorn, the sign before it, and a Leo is actually a Cancerian, its preceding sign. This is the result of misunderstandings and differences in perspectives, and explanations around it are beyond the scope of this book, but can be researched further should you wish to delve a little deeper.

From the astronomical point of view, it is true that the zodiac to which we refer today is not situated where it 'should' be, but indeed, nothing is fixed under the celestial vault. And so the starting point of the ancient zodiac does not correspond exactly to the one we can observe today. But for the purposes of increasing your power and luck, let's keep things simple and enjoy the ride; after all, astrology - while based upon many scientific theories, mysteries, scepticism, superstitions, facts, measurable patterns, ambiguities, correlations, paradoxes, contradictions, links, stigmatisms and observations that seek to support, refute, prove and disprove this ancient art time and again - is ultimately meant to be *fun* too!

THE SUN

Earth's Luminary ★ *Our Brightest Shining Star*

Our Centre, Core Self, Identity & Inner Guiding Light

"Perfect is what I have said of the work of the Sun."
Hermes Trismegistus, The Emerald Tablet

The Sun is our essence, centre, source, ego strength, power, life force, will, vitality, creative expression, purpose, life's direction, our sense of identity, and who we really *are*. Our brightest star is the core of our individuality, our inner guiding light. The Sun is externalising, and represents totality, infinity, eternity, the striving toward and ultimate reaching of one's personal destiny, and *completion* in all areas. It is the creative energising giver of life and the 'father' of the zodiac. It endows us with our inherent creative potential and personal identity - our urge to *create* and to *be*. The Sun is our core self, conscious purpose, our sense of creating something out of our own being. It is the integrated personality and represents the *present*, our greatest Gift. The Sun rules the heart and is thus symbolically the centre of self. Indeed, the Sun *is* the heart and the most commanding presence in our birth chart; the luminary Ruler who governs our essential self and wants to be noticed and appreciated, and above all, to *shine*.

★ KEY WORDS ★

Identity, core self, spirit, life force, power, essence, creativity, higher self, the Father, ego, vitality, pride, individuality, leadership, majesty, inner authority, will, expression, willpower, purpose, the journey, the path and the destiny.

THE SUN ★ THE ULTIMATE SOURCE OF LIFE ON EARTH

Throughout the ages, and indeed since life forms began, the electromagnetic waves generated by the Sun have kept planet Earth habitable for humans, animals, plants and minerals. The Sun is, in fact, the only true source of energy on planet Earth. It provides the perfect amount of energy for plants to synthesise all of the products required for growth and reproduction, which is then stored by plants and ingested by humans and animals who, through many complex processes, utilise these various forms of encapsulated Solar energy - and so the cycle continues. Wood, fuel and minerals (crystals included), too, are merely various forms of this encased Sun energy. In fact, all matter is essentially 'frozen' light. Human body cells are bundles of Sun energy; we couldn't conceive or process a single thought without the molecules of Solar-energised oxygen and glucose.

In essence, the Sun supports the growth of all species, including human beings and microscopic life forms, and without it life on Earth would simply not be possible. The mathematical and metaphysical complexity that stands behind a system of organisation and order so infinitely diverse and intricate as planetary life cannot be truly fathomed, but unerringly and miraculously, the Sun instinctively knows what each species, from a tree to a human, intrinsically needs in order to fulfil its evolutionary purpose and cycles.

Ultimately, the electromagnetic waves generated by the Sun come in a variety of lengths, which determine their specific course of action and responsibility. There are gamma rays, x-rays, cosmic rays, various kinds of ultraviolet rays, infrared, short-wave infrared, radio waves, electric waves, and of course the visible light spectrum, consisting of the seven colour rays.

Most of these energy waves are absorbed and used for various processes in the layers of atmosphere that encircle the Earth, and only a small portion of them - the electromagnetic spectrum - reach the surface of our planet. Although the human eye is only able to perceive about one percent of this spectrum, the waves exert a very strong influence upon us. The waves and rays which do affect us so profoundly, allow all life forms to undergo constant cycles of change necessary for growth and renewal. Physically, we can observe this, but on a deeper, more spiritual plane, we can even *feel* it and allow its radiance to permeate our very souls. Such is the might, force and power of that astonishing ball of fire in our sky: the brilliant, ever-shining Sun.

THE SUN ★ WHAT IT REPRESENTS IN THE HUMAN PSYCHE & NATAL CHART

"The Sun is the most powerful of all the stellar bodies. It colours the personality so strongly that an amazingly accurate picture can be given of the individual who was born when it was exercising its power through the known and predicable influences of a certain astrological sign; these electromagnetic vibrations will continue to stamp that person with the characteristics of their Sun sign as they go through life."
Linda Goodman's Sun Signs, Linda Goodman, Pan Books, 1968

The Sun is our essence, our core self, conscious purpose and sense of identity, our creative potential, our spirit, the integrated personality that shines outward from within us. It is concerned with the present. It is our centre, source, power, life force, will, vitality, purpose, life's direction, what and who we *really* are.

The Sun represents our basic urge for self-expression. It is the 'Solar energy cell' in a person's character, the Lord and giver of life, and symbolises the way in which an individual will shine out to the world. Our Sun is our personal identity and aspects to it from other components in the chart show the ease or otherwise of assuredness and confidence with which one will project and express one's individuality. The Sun sign will also show how an individual bounces back from setbacks and disappointments, their resilience and their general outward expression of energy.

The Sun is the archetype of the Father and represents the primary masculine principle in the natal chart. It indicates how we express and experience our masculine side, or animus, our conscious self, how we express ourselves creatively, our personal potential, individuality, self-expression and personal power. It has to do with courage, power, generosity, creativity, vitality, self-confidence, nobility, self-worth, dignity and strength of will. It symbolises authority and purpose, the *ruler*, and its potential is the peak of constructive maturity. It signifies self-sufficiency and abundance, containing enough energy to radiate warmth and give life to everything around it.

The sign in which one's Sun is posited, and its placement in the birth chart, strongly indicates the level and type of vitality available to the personality (the sign), and in which area of life this may be most strongly directed (the house).

The Sun in a natal chart is a powerful symbol because everything is filtered, at a conscious level, through it. It tells us what we need to do to feel fully alive, the type of engine 'driving' us, what we need to do to be authentic and to be fully functioning. Listening to the special message of one's Sun sign can provide one with greater direction, and a more dynamic energy and life purpose.

While the Moon, the night sky's luminary, represents the *soul*, the Sun, the day sky's luminary, represents our *spirit*.

There is a reason your Sun sign is otherwise known as your Star Sign - it's because, quite simply, the Sun *is* a star; in fact, it's the largest, brightest, shiniest one in Earth's known visible Universe. This book is about your Sun sign and how you can become much larger, glow with far more brilliance, and shine brighter than you ever dreamed possible. I wish you all the magic in the galaxy for your dreams to come true and your deepest wishes to become reality, through tapping into the amazing power and inherent potential of your Sun sign. So get set for a galactical ride through the lucky stars of your constellation - and may a shooting star cross the path in front of you as you go!

LEO THE LION

★ Fixed Fire, Masculine, Positive, Intuitive ★

"Solar energy shines out from my centre"

Body & Health
Heart, Back, Spine, Upper Back, Forearms, Wrists

How Leo Emanates its Life Force / Energy
Extravagantly, brightly, dramatically, with style

Is Concerned With
★ Pleasure ★ Fun ★ Play ★ Entertainment ★
★ Applause, recognition, compliments ★
★ Romances, love affairs, sex ★
★ Charm ★ Children ★ Appreciation ★
★ Gambling, sports, games, taking risks ★
★ Arts ★ Drama ★ Performance ★
★ Leisure ★ Creativity ★ Limelight ★

Spiritual Leo

Your Archetypal Universal Qualities
The Leader, Golden Child, Performer

What You Refuse
To accept no for an answer, to submit, or to take a backseat in life

What You Are an Authority On
Generosity, chivalry, spirit, creativity, play, charm

The Main Senses Through Which You Experience Your Reality
Ego, centeredness, warmth, love, playfulness, creative expression

How You Love
Vigorously, with affection

Positive Characteristics
★ Honest ★ Generous ★ Loyal ★
★ Hospitable ★ Dignified ★ Affectionate ★
★ Accepting of people at face value ★
★ Courage ★ Sunny Disposition ★
★ Proud ★ Warm and Loving ★
★ Lively ★ Vibrant ★ Demonstrative ★
★ Enthusiastic ★ Positive ★ Encouraging ★

Negative Characteristics
★ Stubborn ★ Wilful ★ Overbearing ★ Vain ★
★ Takes Undue Credit ★ Condescending ★
★ Cold-hearted when Hurt ★ ★ Excessively Proud ★
★ Cuts Others Down to Size ★ Bossy ★
★ Sulky ★ Childish ★ Boastful, smug ★
★ Controlling ★ Arrogant ★ Contemptuous ★
★ Attention-grabbing ★ Dominating ★

To Bring Out Your Best
Throw lavish parties; involve yourself with children; make time for play and leisure; buy and wear

expensive gold jewellery, attend acting classes, write and star in your own play.

Spiritual Goals

To learn to share the stage and attract more genuine appreciation and respect; to be more authentic; to lower your expectations of others; to use your natural flair for leadership by encouraging others to shine too; to be more modest and endearing by toning down your attention-seeking.

LEO

23 July - 22 August

Fixed Fire

Ruled by the Sun

"I WILL"

Gemstones ◊ Citrine, Ruby, Peridot

★ Warm-hearted, expansive, enthusiastic, arrogant, dynamic, extravagant, direct, loyal, pompous, loving, creative, regal, confident, driven, bold,
generous, affectionate, honest, dignified, powerful, noble, playful, bossy, attention-seeking, demanding, vain, dramatic, protective, dominating, proud, promiscuous, overbearing, magnanimous,
leader, conceited, fun, chivalrous, wholehearted, ostentatious, stubborn, strong-willed, naïve, affected, determined, fearless, ambitious, presumptuous, pushy, daring, brave, imperious ★

"I have the same goal I've had ever since I was a girl.
I want to rule the world"
Madonna

LEO

♌

★ Charming ★ Noble ★ Generous ★
★ Warm ★ Affectionate ★ Dramatic ★
★ Vain ★ Dignified

Leo is the sign of the Lion, the (often self-declared) 'King of the Jungle', a regal and magnificent animal who rules over the pride and expects it to cater to his every demand. Vain, bossy, arrogant, warm, playful, good-humoured, driven, dynamic, attention-seeking, dramatic, confident, dignified and noble are Leos' most notable traits. Being of the fabulous Fire element, your sign burns brightly and warmly, but can become overbearing and bossy in your constant need for attention and centre stage position. Confident and dominating, Leo loves to lead and is easily seduced by flattery and compliments, which he just as readily gives to others.

The Lion is enthusiastic and generous to a fault, always willing to give someone the shirt off their backs or their last dollar, but only if it doesn't compromise their own comforts, ego needs, indulgences and extravagances. The larger than life Leo craves attention and adoration, but his pride is easily hurt and he will retreat temporarily to lick his wounds if he loses a battle. Being a Fixed sign, loyalty is a big thing for the big-hearted Lion's spirit, and his loyalty in friendship and love is second to none! A hearty and affectionate lover, loyal and fun-loving friend and playful performer in the dance of life, Leo is the fifth sign and the all-powerful King of the zodiac, winning people over and lighting the way with his commanding presence, powerful personality, warm nature and luminous spirit.

KEY CONCEPTS
★ Vain and self-seeking ★
★ Falsely modest ★
★ Egotistical, braggart and show-off ★
★ Bossy and dictatorial ★
★ Affected by flattery and compliments ★
★ Refined, composed, proud and cultivated ★
★ Indiscriminately embracing of others ★
★ Hedonistic, lustful and pleasure-seeking ★
★ Self-assured and forward-moving ★
★ Extravagant and opulent ★
★ Gregarious, affectionate and sociable ★
★ Artistic, dramatic and expressive ★
★ Cleverly creative ★
★ Sincere, warm, inspired and inspiring ★

SOME CORRESPONDENCES THAT ARE ASSOCIATED WITH LEO

Gold, courtship, theatres, resorts, fame, entertainment, monarchs, royalty, amusement, bosses, power and influence, sport, speculation, directors, pleasure, organisers, romance, managers, creativity, social clubs, crowns, superiors, stage performers, gambling, casinos, governments, playgrounds, games, the heart, the limelight, matchmaking, sunrooms, the first child, oranges, VIPs, theatrical life, spotlights, warmth and leadership. Take your pick and enjoy the ride!

QUOTES BY LEONINES

"Too much of a good thing can be wonderful" - Mae West (17 August 1893)

"I don't believe, I *know*" - Carl G. Jung (26 July 1875)

"My work in books, films and talks lies almost wholly with children, and I have very little time to give to grown-ups" - Enid Blyton (11 August 1897)

"For me, life is continuously being hungry. The meaning of life is not simply to exist, to survive, but to move ahead, to go up, to achieve, to conquer" - Arnold Schwarzenegger (30 July 1947)

"Thank goodness I was never sent to school; it would have rubbed off some of the originality" - Beatrix Potter (28 July 1866)

"A girl should be two things: classy and fabulous" - Coco Chanel (19 August 1883)

"All kids need is a little help, a little hope and somebody who believes in them" - Magic Johnson (14 August 1959)

"I knew I was a winner back in the late sixties. I knew I was destined for great things. People will say that kind of thinking is totally immodest. I agree. Modesty is not a word that applies to me in any way. I hope it never will" - Arnold Schwarzenegger

"I find capitalism repugnant. It is filthy, it is gross, it is alienating … because it causes war, hypocrisy and competition" - Fidel Castro (13 August 1926)

"I am a part of all that I have read" - John Kieran (2 August 1892)

"Smoking is related to practically every terrible thing that can happen to you" - Loni Anderson (5 August 1946)

"All outward forms of religion are almost useless, and are causes of endless strife … (just) behave yourself and never mind the rest" - Beatrix Potter

"I was never a good student. I had to be dragged into kindergarten. It was hard to sit and listen to somebody talk. I wanted to be out, educated by experience and adventure" - Robert Redford (18 August 1936)

"I am a businessman. This is what I do each and every day. I love it. I love coming to work. I never have a bad day" - Magic Johnson

"I am not young but I feel young … J'aime la vie! I feel that to live is a wonderful thing" - Coco Chanel

"A leader is a dealer in hope" - Napoleon Bonoparte (15 August 1769)

"I stand for freedom of expression, doing what you believe in, and going after your dreams" - Madonna (16 August 1958)

"Money doesn't make you happy. I now have $50 million but I was just as happy when I had $48 million" - Arnold Schwarzenegger

"Thinking is the hardest work there is. Which is the probably reason why so few people engage in it" - Henry Ford (30 July 1863)

"For me personally, skiing holds everything … it's a complete physical expression of freedom" - Robert Redford

"I began revolution with 82 men. If I had to do it again, I do it with 10 or 15 and absolute faith. It does not matter how small you are if you have faith and plan of action" - Fidel Castro

"My fellow Americans, we are and always will be a nation of immigrants. We were strangers once, too" - Barrack Obama (4 August 1961)

"There is something inherently valuable about being a misfit … there is definitely a value for identifying yourself differently and being proud that you are different" - Daniel Radcliffe (23 July 1989)

"In order to be irreplaceable one must always be different" - Coco Chanel

"You only live once, but if you do it right, once is enough" - Mae West

"I often quote myself. It adds spice to the conversation" - George Bernard Shaw (26 July 1856)

"I don't want to live. I want to love first and live incidentally" - Zelda Fitzgerald (24 July 1900)

"At the moment I am looking into astrology … There are strange and wondrous things in these lands of darkness. Please, don't worry about my wanderings in these infinitudes. I shall return laden with rich booty for our knowledge of the human psyche" - Carl G. Jung

"Change will not come if we wait for some other person or some other time. We are the ones we've been waiting for. We are the change that we seek" - Barrack Obama

"I never worry about diets. The only carrots that interest me are the number you get in a diamond" - Mae West

"Take me or leave me, or, as in the usual order of things, both" - Dorothy Parker (22 August 1893)

"We were born at a given moment, in a given place, and like vintage years of wine, we have the qualities of the year and of the season in which we are born" - Carl G. Jung

"I am my own experiment. I am my own work of art" - Madonna

"The secret of staying young is to live honestly, eat slowly, and lie about your age" - Lucille Ball

"I am a deeply superficial person" - Andy Warhol (6 August 1928)

"All men dream, but not equally. Those who dream by night in the dusty recesses of their minds wake in the day to find that it was vanity: but the dreamers of the day are dangerous men, for they may act their dream with open eyes, to make it possible" - T.E. Lawrence

"As we all know, science began with the stars, and mankind in them the dominants of the unconscious, the 'gods', as well as the curious psychological qualities of the zodiac: a complete projected theory of human character" - Carl G. Jung

"Lack of money is the root of all evil" - George Bernard Shaw

"I don't know much about being a millionaire, but I bet I'd be a darling at it" - Dorothy Parker

"If I had ten years left to live, I would spend it studying astrology" - Carl G. Jung

THE LEO CONSTELLATION

The signs of the zodiac are the twelve symbolic features that ancient people imagined while observing the heavens. They saw shapes, patterns, faces, and natural and supernatural beings in the stars, from which they established, over centuries, a kind of celestial hierarchy and system based upon their observations. Groupings of stars became constellations, and twelve of these constellations make up the zodiac, a Greek word meaning 'circle of animals', that we know today.

Star constellations are not really self-contained groups but are particularly bright stars that give the appearance of being close together and form distinctive patterns. These are the patterns that over the ages have been identified as animals, deities or mythological figures and heroes. The stars are the living past. We receive their light long after it has left the star itself and so they are a good focus for escaping from the parameters of time. Their stellar influence is analogous with the aura, the bio/psychic energy field surrounding humans, animals, plants, crystals and even places. These individual energy systems interact with the energy waves emanated by other people, and even the cosmic rays emitted by planetary bodies, for psychic energies are not limited by time or distance.

The cluster of stars we know as Leo the Lion, are bright and form a shape vaguely resembling an animal like a lion, for Northern Hemisphere viewers - in the Southern Hemisphere it is seen upside down.

The Lion's mane is said to be featured in the pattern of stars, and in Leo's glyph. Leo contains a very bright star called Regulus (Latin for 'little king'), so named by Copernicus, also known as the Heart of the Lion, which sits right on the ecliptic, and which is very significant astrologically. Because it is so bright and luminous, Regulus is often mistaken for a planet.

An extremely bright and easily identifiable constellation, the most recognisable feature of the constellation is his 'mane', which looks like a large question mark or huge sickle, at which the base is Regulus, the heart of the lion. Often depicted in a crouching position, as if preparing to leap, the body of the Lion forms a rectangle of less prominent but still noticeable stars, and culminates in the triangle of the Lion's hindquarters. The constellation's 'tail' is long and curved, the tip of which is a blue star known as Denebola. The Leo constellation can be spotted in the sky by first locating the Big Dipper, for Leo's head is found just under its giant ladle.

WISHING UPON YOUR STAR

The practice of wishing upon a star is familiar to most of us, and is a mystical superstition that is ingrained in many of us from childhood. As a night-time ritual, you can wish upon your own sign's constellation or that of the sign whose energies you wish to call forth; indeed, you can wish upon any constellation you feel an affinity with. If you can't see a particular constellation in your night sky, you can always meditate on it in your mind, or you can use the traditional technique of wishing upon the first star you see, while reciting the popular rhyme: *Star light, star bright, first star I see tonight, I wish I may, I wish I might, have the wish I make this night!* Any one of the three rituals will hold power for your own special wish. Good luck!

THE LEONINE SYMBOL ♌

Astrology uses symbols or 'glyphs' to represent the planets and signs. The glyph is made up of shapes representing the energy and physical matter of which the Universe is composed, and how these shapes are used in each symbol provide hints as to the properties of the sign or planet it represents.

The ancient view was that there were five elements: Fire, Water, Air, Earth and Ether (or Spirit). Ether is invisible energy, while the four tangible elements are known as 'matter'. Ether, as pure energy, cannot be influenced by any of the physical/matter elements, although it surrounds them and indeed fuels them. The Greek philosopher and scientist Aristotle regarded this idea as a circle (Ether/Spirit) with a cross (matter) in the centre. This glyph is used in astrology as a symbol for Earth, and the cycle of life. All the symbols used in astrology represent the relationship between energy and the 'matter' elements.

The glyph of Leo is a little more obscure than those of the previous four signs before it. It represents the serpent power (creative force) of the body in its coiled (latent) form. The lion is the undisputed king in his own sphere and is noted for his great strength and ferocity when roused, as difficult to cope with as the human passions when unrestrained. Celebrities are 'lionised' or looked upon as social 'lions', and are also affectionately labelled as 'the cat's whiskers'. The full heat of the Sun * in Leo ripens the corn for harvest in Virgo.

Leo's symbol is also represented by a kind of distorted hook, but in many interpretations is said to be a Lion's tail or a Lion's mane.

* In the Northern Hemisphere's summer

THE AGE OF LEO ★ 10,000 - 8000 BC

The Age of Leo is the earliest time of human culture that we can speculate about, and heralded a golden period of heightened imagination and creativity. All indications suggest that it was the height of Sun worship, Leo's planetary ruler. The Sun was of crucial importance during this time, as it increased in strength, marking the end of the Ice Age. The first sign of humanity's involvement with art can be found in the primitive cave paintings that date from this period. Leo is the sign of creativity and expression and therefore has a special association with painting. Early paint colours were made from ochre, which could be crushed and manipulated to create shades of red and yellow - colours associated with both the Sun and Leo. Many historians believe that the Egyptian Sphinx and the pyramids were built around the time of the Age of Leo. Indeed, aligned with the constellation of Leo, the Sphinx's commanding image possesses the rear body and tail of a Lion.

THE RUNDOWN & LESSONS
SOME QUIRKS, ODDITIES, UNIQUE
CHARACTERISTICS AND IDIOSYNCRASIES OF
LEO

With pride the Lion lifts his mane
And takes a look at his wide domain
He knows that he must rule with might
Yet ever so gently with Love and Light
Alan Oken

"To subdue him, simply flatter him. His vanity is his Achilles' heel ... Leo is a fiercely loyal friend, a just but powerful enemy, creative and original, strong and vital - whether he's a quiet or a flamboyant lion, for there are both kinds. We overlook his arrogance, his sometimes insufferable ego, his rather ridiculous spells of vanity and laziness, because his heart, like his metal, is pure gold."
Linda Goodman

There are two types of thinkers: what I like to call 'right-brainers' and 'left-brainers'. The left hemisphere of the human brain deals with things such as control of speech, verbal functions, logic, reason, mathematics, linear concepts, details, sequences, the intellect and analysis; the right hemisphere is concerned with spatial, music, holistic, artistic concepts, as well as simultaneity and intuition. You could go on to say that the left brain is masculine or yang in quality, and the right brain is feminine or yin in quality. Based upon these very simplistic outlines, it can be further stated that Fire sign Leo dwells mainly in the left hemisphere, with a healthy dose of right thrown in for good measure.

The enthusiastic nature of Fire highlights inspiration, action and impulse. Leo is largely motivated by its ego and inspired fixity of purpose. Positive, hot, dry, masculine, choleric and hearty, a determined (Fixed) optimistic (Fire) approach characterises the sign of Leo.

Like his jungle counterpart in the animal kingdom, Leo truly is the King of the zodiac. And in the same way that Leo's ruler, the Sun, outshines and overpowers all other lights, the magnitude of Leo's personality blazes out as he stands, centre stage of whatever platform he chooses to step up to or occupy in life. It has to be said first and foremost that Leo is definitely not a wallflower, but ever a Sunflower. Leo is the second of the Fiery signs, is positive in magnetism, and is ruled by our mighty Solar Star. People born under this sign are generally enthusiastic, dramatic, idealistic and generous, directing their energies to develop a genuine self-hood, presenting their confident egos on the world stage, and taking pride and finding pleasure in the creative accomplishments that are the healthy expression of individual self-discovery.

The Fixed nature of the Leo character implies solidity and confidence, while its Fire element adds warmth and enthusiasm. The Lion is known as the King of the Beasts, displaying this sovereignty with a relaxed charisma and style. Fixed Fire is like an eternal flame and Leo is gifted with an abundance of ever-radiating heat and power through its benevolence, wisdom and magnanimity. Courageous, magnetic, exuberant, with a flair for leadership and an innate desire to play, Leos express a warmth which uplifts others and inspires confidence, as long as they can keep their place in the spotlight and upon their thrones. And this they do well, for it seems that nothing can topple them from their majestic jewelled golden chair. Negative qualities can rise to the surface at times, such as conceit, over-extravagance, vanity, arrogance, pretentiousness, boastfulness, domination, an incessant need for approval and validation, and the shadow side of their natural courage - cowardice.

The Lion is a strong symbol for Leo, standing quite literally for the Monarch of the Kingdom, and if a Leo roars loudly, it can intimidate and scare off everyone and everything around it. But usually not for long. There is something inherently childlike and buoyant about this big pussycat, even when they *are* being bossy, domineering and overbearing. You believe yourself to be special and go out of your way to receive the full VIP treatment from others. This you usually achieve as others fall for your charm and guile. Plus, you are naïve, trusting and approachable, so there's not much not to love about your spirit. People also gravitate towards your integrity and loyalty, like bees to honey - and your creativity radiates far and wide, touching all those with whom you come into contact deeply. You have the power to affect and to influence, and you usually go to great lengths to utilise this talent. Indeed, if your occasional snobbishness and wilfulness are softened, you can be highly successful in all life areas.

There is nothing modest about Leo; he's a very efficient self-promoter and likes to be appreciated for his efforts and uniqueness. You derive pleasure from your magnanimity and your capacity for enjoyment is rarely affected by the trials and tribulations of everyday living. In essence, your zest for life and appreciation of pleasure is unequalled by any other sign.

There is also not a lot of sharing about Leo. The realm of the Fifth House of the astrological mandala, over which you naturally rule and reside in, is where we learn that we have the ability to become what we want to be; we start to value ourselves as independent beings. Note that there is no evidence of sharing in this. Sharing implies equality of rights, and Leo does not acknowledge, nor is concerned, with equality. You may bestow, graciously and kindly; you may give greatly of your big heart; you may display warm solicitude for those who place themselves under your protection; as much as you love the good life, you may even deny yourself in order to gratify a loved one's wants. But these are not acts of *sharing* per se. His Majesty will take care of his subjects, only so long as they recognise his sovereignty. Despite this very well-disguised lack of sharing in its pure sense, people will instinctively be drawn to you for counsel, for friendship, for a smile or even just a pat on the back. And you give it all! By the strength and essence of your self-approval and confidence, you create a sort of magnetic field which pulls people into the experience of your uplifting and lovable company. An old astrology text illustrates a fine example of this seemingly effortless gravitational pull: "As the planets revolve around the Sun, as the Lion snoozes while his wives are out catching a zebra for his supper, so is Leo most in tune with life while he's sitting quietly in the midst of his admirers."

Content though you often are, especially when surrounded by your worshippers, you are not always calm of mind and spirit. Being a Fixed sign, it is virtually impossible to get you to change your mind. You are direct and like to think in straight lines, and any opinions formed when you are young and impressionable are usually held firmly into old age. Unlike the other two Fire signs Aries and Sagittarius, you are not impulsive, but rather deliberate in your thinking and targeted in your approach. You give important matters their due consideration and respect, but details tend to be overlooked and decisions that are reached tend to be based on intuition or a 'hunch' rather than deep contemplation, fact or intellect.

You are an extremely proud creature - and indeed, you have many qualities in which you can justly take pride: you're generous of spirit, charismatic, larger than life, loving and creative. But pride can also be your downfall. You find it almost impossible to admit you may be wrong about something, and pride combined with your Fixed nature can create obstinacy and pomposity. Your Achilles heel is your vanity, for your craving to be permanently under the spotlight and your constant need for admiration, can for the most part attract only superficial flattery from others - and blinded by conceit, you're easily manipulated by the unscrupulous. In this respect, you are extremely gullible. You can be almost ruined by flattery, and completely stopped in your tracks by a compliment, thereby cultivating the wrong kind of acquaintance, who may take advantage of your naïve, impressionable nature. But allowances can be made for you, for if you are a show-off it is because you have been the centre of attention all your life; and if you are cocky, it's because you're multi-talented and can therefore actually back up your claims; if you are bossy, it is because you are actually the best one to be in charge. In any case, the Lion is authentic and only believes his own hype because it is, under all the frills and roar, *true*. You are honest above all else, and don't hide yourself behind mysterious or tricky facades. What you see is what you get with the ever-inflated Lion.

Leo also holds true to his promises. With his charm, charisma, and a Leonine touch of arrogance, he will promise you the world - and deliver it without ado. He can - and frequently does - move mountains. And when it comes to romance, you wrote the book, your tender and skilful artistry in all things love will leave your lovers starry-eyed and feeling cherished and adored. For you are deeply sentimental, generously affectionate and warmly loving. But you are prone to jealousy and possessiveness, and must come first in your loved one's affections, focus and attentions.

Creative and resourceful, you are the most determined of all the Fire signs. Your ambitious goals and theatrical impact upon the world give you a reputation which make you a person to be admired and followed. When you curb your will to dominate and respect the individuality of others, your success and happiness will increase accordingly. With your inner Fire, you can make your life an inspiring artistic masterpiece which enthuses, enriches and invokes reverence from others.

The astrological meaning of Leo is in accordance with the seasonal time of the year (in the Northern Hemisphere) when the Sun is at its brightest. The Sun during its most luminous month is analogous to being the central figure, or in the position of leader in society. As the visible symbol of the life-force which animates all sentient beings, and signifies the vital power or energy at the core of our existence, the Sun is a fitting rulership for the Lion, the King of them all. This Solar force is of itself neither good nor bad; it is simply pure, unadulterated power. But if allowed to run wild without conscious direction, it can lead to urges to dominate, bully and conquer, or the rampant egotism which Leo is so well-known for.

Your paradox can lie in your need for approval and praise from others and your insatiable desire to rule over them, but you are mortified if you yourself are ever reduced to asking for help, money, encouragement or advice. You love to be accepted by others, yet oddly like to remain independent of mind and spirit. You have enough ego to keep you buoyed, ample confidence to fuel your own motivation, sufficient enthusiasm to keep your Fires burning, and enough wisdom to accumulate your own gold, so thankfully you rarely have to ask anyone from your pride for assistance.

Very proud, ambitious and strong-willed, with a tendency to show off generally and be extroverted in dress, you stand out from the crowd - not necessarily through unique quirks as is the case with your opposite sign Aquarius, but because you command it with your manner and attire. You are vain, ardent, and able to organise and to lead, with a notorious and marked ability for arts and drama. You are extremely astute and will never waste your energy flogging a dead horse or trying to get water from a dry well as other more idealistic signs might, which makes you a superb organiser and a wise delegator of duties. In fact, so good is your ability to command and organise - and because you are such a master of straightforward, direct communication - your demands are always met and your leadership is always effective. You also have an uncanny knack and impressive genius for being able to evade messy or unpleasant tasks, and are more than happy to compensate others generously for doing these things for you while you attend to the more important matters of preening yourself, radiating sunrays and looking beautiful.

Your path being guided by the Sun, you seek success and illumination. The Solar gods of mythology had the task of lighting up the world, and you too, have this task - as well as the power to pull it off. Your presence and radiance sometimes burn so brightly that lesser mortals may feel frazzled by your grandiosity, but the Sun can also teach you to burn steadily, then rest and rise again.

Love you or loathe you, there's no overlooking the Lion. Whatever you say, you usually mean with all your heart. Your Fire can warm and soothe others or singe them, but in any case it never fails to leave an indelible impression. Whether you're a roaring Lion or purring pussycat, your mission in life is to make your mark with style and panache, and this you rarely fail to accomplish.

LESSONS TO BE LEARNED FOR GREATER POWER, ENLIGHTENMENT & LUCK

Leonine problems and ultimate undoings arise through your bossiness, grabbing at attention, pride, extravagance and arrogance. Your tendency to want to 'rule' over others can develop into a compulsive need to control and be in the spotlight. More modest signs may feel intimidated but you would never know, due to your Fixed nature, stubbornness and blinders conveniently blocking your view. Although generous to a fault, you may exploit others' weaknesses and (unwittingly or perhaps not) dictate how they should live their lives. You need to recognise the true power of your influence over others, and lead without being bossy, compel without exploiting, and love unconditionally, without the expectation of adoration and constant praise from others.

All your strengths spring from an abundance of vital, affectionate energy and from a generosity of heart and spirit. At your shining best, you love life with such direct and bold passion, and pour so much creative energy into your worldly commitments, that the world recognises, applauses and rewards you accordingly. However, at your worst, you can become self-obsessed and bullish, and demand attention and congratulations for even inept half-hearted efforts. Your endless pride, when based upon self-respect and joy, leads to strength of purpose, courage and success, but when that same pride grows from a seed of insecurity, arrogance or fear, empty vanity, escapism or tyrannical behaviour can result. With so much vitality to positively radiate, the Lion's inborn strengths can easily flourish, and when you come from your true centre, *real* magic can happen.

THE THREE DECANS OF LEO

Decans are thirty-six groups of stars that rise in a particular order on the horizon throughout each Earth rotation. These decans were developed in Egypt thousands of years ago. The rising of each decan marked the beginning of a new 'decanal hour' of the night for these ancient people, and eventually three decans were assigned to each zodiac sign. Each decan covers ten degrees of the zodiac wheel, and is ruled by different planetary rulers that rule over the other two signs of the same element (and a traditional ruler, when only seven of the planetary bodies were known). Decans continued to be used throughout the Ages, in astrology and in magic, but many modern astrologers, for whatever reasons, tend to disregard them. Following are brief descriptions for each decan of Leo. Which one do you belong to? Can you relate to the description and the energies of your decan's ruling planet?

FIRST DECAN LEO ★ July 23 - August 2

Ruler ★ Saturn (traditional *) / Sun (modern)

Keyword ★ Extreme

First Decan Leos' Three Special Tarot Cards
Strength, King of Wands & Five of Wands

Birthdays in this decan range from 23rd July to 2nd August. This is the Leo decan, ruled by Saturn * and the Sun. Leos born during this decan possess fiery passions and a wilful temperament. You have a healthy appetite for ambition and power, and have great leadership skills, which you probably use to great effect. You may however, have a constant desire to dominate, or exercise control or authority over others, and although your ability to lead and succeed is strong, you are at frequent risk of despotism, authoritarianism, egocentrism and excessive pride. If you put your strengths to good use, you are likely to achieve success, fame and social recognition. Enthusiastic and vital, you are gifted with great talents. Independent, gregarious and creative, you love the limelight and are at your best when in the public arena. You also have a highly sensitive ego which is easily bruised, so you dislike relying on anyone or anything, preferring to carve your own path and reap your own self-made - and well-deserved! - rewards. With a love of a buzz of activity around you, you have a distaste for being idle, but this makes you prone to being a workaholic and unable to relax.

SECOND DECAN LEO ★ August 3 - 12

Ruler ★ Jupiter (traditional *) / Jupiter (modern)

Keyword ★ Confident

Second Decan Leos' Three Special Tarot Cards
Strength, King of Wands & Six of Wands

Birthdays in this decan range from 3rd August to 12th August. You were born in the second decan of Leo, and your planetary ruler is Jupiter. Jupiter is said to be the harbinger of riches, religion, good fortune, travel, gains, philosophy, social position and status. Naturally, this makes you a lover of all the beautiful and good things life has to offer, and you radiate cheer, optimism and inspiration. Possessing a great sense of humour, you are a natural entertainer with a lifelong love of learning and a fondness for travelling, broadening your horizons and seizing opportunities. You are an eternal optimist and in turn, attract good luck and fortune wherever you go or whatever you choose to do. You may also possess an exaggerated self-confidence and an indulgent streak with little fear of consequences. Generous to a fault, you may be impulsive and ostentatiously extravagant. Your heart is as big as your life, and you often try to live above your means due to your desire to be admired or approved of. Expansion is your noblest aim, and you seek this for yourself and others.

THIRD DECAN LEO ★ August 13 - 22

Ruler ★ Mars (traditional *) / Mars (modern)

Keyword ★ Powerful

Third Decan Leos' Three Special Tarot Cards
Strength, Knight of Pentacles & Seven of Wands

Birthdays in this decan range from 13th August to 22nd August. This is the Aries decan, ruled by Mars *. Leos born during this decan are characterised by a driven, intense, arduous desire to succeed. Purposeful, forceful, passionate and determined, you are illuminated by your own bright lights. The Mars influence can make you impetuous, impulsive, egotistical and bold, often full of bluster and bravado. You may suffer an inflated self-confidence, but this confidence may indeed be justified, as you are usually fearless, dynamic, direct and ambitious. You tend to set high goals and ideals for yourself, but always seem to have the audacity and zeal to attain them. Straightforward and bossy, you may be too honest for some people, and alienate them with your blunt and tactless tongue.

The decan's traditional ruler based on the Chaldean order of the planets

YOUR ELEMENT ★ FIRE

According to the *Oxford English Dictionary*, the word *element* has a mysterious origin, and was first found in Greek texts meaning 'complex whole' or 'a single unit made up of many parts'. From the ancient up to medieval times, there were only four elements - Earth, Air, Fire and Water - and the occult-oriented also believed in a fifth: Spirit, or Ether. (Cornelius Agrippa called Spirit the 'quintessence'.)

Alchemy is a tradition of visions and dreams, and images can combine on different levels of reality. Alchemists have long used images in their illustrations to express the enigma and mystery of their art, and to include all dimensions of our experience. The traditional worlds of Earth, Water, Fire and Air symbolise these dimensions very well. Broadly speaking, and in human terms, Earth corresponds to the level of the body and the senses, Water to the flow of thoughts and feelings, Fire to inspiration and energy, and Air to the world of the higher mind and intellect. Each of these worlds has its own realm of imagery. Leo belongs to the realm of the Fire element.

★ The Passionate Group ★

The path to INSPIRATION

Focused on Identity & Action

Alchemical Associations ★ Transformation, Sulphur and the Colour Red

Key Attributes ★ Energy, passion, decisiveness, illumination, expansion

Symbolism ★ Clear thought, communication, study, connection to the Universals

Governed by ★ The Spirit and Intuition

Fire Characteristics ★ Passionate, energetic, courageous, wild, vibrant, transformational

★ THE MAGIC OF FIRE ★

Fire is the fuel that drives willpower and gives you the energy you need to turn your dreams into reality. Beware, however, as fire can easily flare out of control. Powerful, dynamic and constantly changing, it is difficult to contain and control, but when used wisely it brings light, warmth and hope to your experience. Without the action fire drives, you would stay grounded and uninspired - rooted to the spot forever. Fire brings your desires into fruition by bringing determination and bravery - a natural call to action.

★ KEYWORDS ★

Adventurous, energetic, ardent, independent, passionate, enthusiastic, optimistic, impulsive, honest, exuberant, self-motivated, physical, individualistic, assertive, inspirational, courageous, has faith, spirited, warm, takes initiative, confident, extroverted, spontaneous, impatient, restless, simple and direct in approach, creative, idealistic, freedom-seeking, dramatic, forceful, Joi de Vivre! *

* All these words don't necessarily describe all three Fire signs. Leo, for example, is not necessarily restless or freedom-seeking.

Fire is fundamentally different to the other three elements, but it is the essential fourth. The other elements are eternal - only Fire has a birth and a death. Fire is ephemeral; even the blazing, glowing ball in the sky, our Sun, will burn out in time. Remember also that you need to nurture and replenish this primal force of expression, as Fire is not self-sustaining and it needs fuel to maintain its heat, light, movement and momentum. Fire is, quite simply, the element of creation, the life force made manifest. The most active and consuming astrological energy, it is the element of spirit, roaming far and wide in search of inspiration and meaning. Fire is also the identity principle. It animates, transmutes and energises.

Fire is associated with the intuitive function and its motivating force is inspiration. Characterised by movement, force and energy, it offers new possibilities, regeneration and a buoyant, spontaneous expression. Fire's essential characteristic is the energetic exploration of life: to conquer, to lead and to travel - both mentally and physically. Fire signs are creative and perceptive, experiencing life through intuition and spirit. Fire is a conceptual and visionary element, ever searching for meaning. Its energy can light up the world, or scorch it out of existence.

Stimulating and spontaneous, it has a warm, passionate, enthusiastic and active approach to life. Fire initiates and motivates, and it is optimistic and explorative. Fire is also connected with heroism, a sense of beginning, regrowth and the future. Aries represents personal development, Leo represents interpersonal development, and Sagittarius represents transpersonal development. They are masculine polarity, extroverted in action.

Fire is strength, power, protection, and the ability to change from one state to another. It is enlightenment and extremely potent but, like Air, it can represent truth and knowledge through purification. The alchemical sigil for Fire is an upright triangle, a male symbol meaning action and movement. Pointing upwards, it represents the path to higher truths, light and transformation through self-motivated activity. But like any magical elemental energy, Fire has two sides: creation and destruction. It can destroy things for the better, such as the symbolic 'burning away' of old thought patterns, bad habits, negativity, and things we no longer need in our lives.

The Fire element is spiritual, progressive, transcending, visionary, confident, 'birthing', associated with starting points, and a sense of the Divine, is reactive, has faith, philosophical, quests for purpose, is playful, joyful, connected to the 'inner child', ascending, optimistic, combative, has a strong expression of emotions, is straightforward, direct, spontaneous, risk-taking, passionate, forceful, dynamic, bold, humorous, idealistic, and intuitive in the perceiving sense, not the feeling sense.

As the element suggests, Fire signs are a great source of warmth, intensity and light, but they can also be volatile. Exuberant, passionate and motivated, Fire signs are the active people of the zodiac, preferring to lead and take initiative rather than wait for things to happen. Blessed with confident, fun-loving and dynamic personalities, they have a natural flair for boosting talent, morale and confidence, and are usually the driving force behind relationship and family decisions. Fire signs are the extroverts of the zodiac, being charismatic, enthusiastic and assertive, usually being the first to make an introduction, explore wider horizons or conquer new ground. While their natural positivity and optimism can be infectious, they may also be inadvertently selfish, overbearing, bossy and over-zealous in their approach. The passionate Fire signs also like stimulation and drama, and in the absence of excitement, may wander elsewhere to find it. Being impulsive, they may take risks and be compelled to act and speak without thinking, coming across as reckless, careless and tactless. Although honest and direct, they may have a tendency to be blunt. Charming but impatient and impetuous, Fire signs have an admirable lust for life, immense bravery, enormous generosity of spirit, and a fierce and protective loyalty towards their loved ones.

"To be alive is to be burning," asserted psychoanalyst Norman O. Brown. Too much burning, however, can lead to burnout. Too much unrestrained Fire can burn others. When Fire people are out of control, fire extinguishers (water) and stamping it out with a heavy material (Earth) can work wonders. Fire generated by a spark can spread as a forest fire spreads, creating excessive heat and smoke, which can sear and smother.

However, the inner heat that Fire provides is the sustaining life force that contributes to self-confidence, radiance, eagerness, faith, forward movement and healthy creative and sexual expressions. Psychologically, Fire is naturally in motion, catalysing inner light, spirituality and vision. Being an inspirational element, it rises upwards and moves forward, and requires space to expand. Its positive expressions are warming, brightening, uplifting and motivating.

> "Suddenly, the whole orchard was ablaze with light, as if the Sun had risen at midnight.
> It was the Firebird. The Firebird had come, with wings that shone like gold and eyes that gleamed like crystal ... (The feather the Firebird left behind) was so glorious that the king immediately forgot about his orchard. The feather was full of brilliance, like a thousand candles all alight at once."
> **Edited extract from *Prince Ivan and the Firebird***

As illustrated in the passage above, the fiery spark that sets the process of creation going is personified in a number of mythological fiery creatures. The salamander living in the flames in our emblem is one such. Many of them are birds, like the legendary Phoenix, the mighty bird of Fire which arises from the ashes. There is also the Simurgh, bird of Divine Light in Asian mythology, and the Sun-bird of ancient Lycia, which takes souls and flies them up to the sky after death.

The Firebird, a miraculous animal from Russian folklore, as the previous extract outlines, is the bird of inspiration. It has been said its feathers shine as if made from silver and gold and its eyes sparkle like crystals. It sits upon a golden perch and, at midnight, illuminates gardens and fields as brightly as a thousand lights. When the Firebird sings, pearls fall from its break and the sound has the power to heal the sick. It feeds on golden apples which have the power to endow immortality and beauty to those who eat them. A single feather from its tail will light a room; and one feather from her tail is said to be enough to set you off on a Quest. Fire can indeed set us ablaze with enthusiasm. Sometimes it must be seized with both hands, and once the Fire is ignited, it demands action, energy and risk-taking. Fire is not just for the chosen few, for we all have a chance to find a spark and use it; but once discovered, it demands decisive commitment.

According to the I Ching, the hexagram li/li, fire over fire, suggests that, "A luminous thing giving out light must have within itself something that perseveres; otherwise it will burn itself out."

Fire is crucial to alchemy, because heat is a key agent in transformation. Fire also effects colour changes, another critical component of the alchemical process. Further, most of us have some significant memory, fascination, fear, wonder, nervousness or curiosity about fire. Fire can quickly get out of control, and as such careful regulation of it is crucial, both literally and metaphorically in terms of our own enthusiasm. It can destroy, but for all its destruction, it can provide the perfect conditions for the seeds of new life to spring forth. Fire must be controlled however, for enthusiasm is a useful tool but a terrible master, as it drives out discernment and discrimination.

Red, yellow and orange are the colours associated with Fire, and other associations include the Sun, candles, lanterns, swords, warfare, wands, volcanoes, beacons, torches, salamanders, rams, lions, dragons and phoenixes.

Fire comes from the Sun, our great 'Father' in the sky whose warmth and radiance uplifts us all. As followers upon a magical path, we must possess a Fire within us too - a Fire of vision which brings in its wake strong and true wisdom. For when we are carriers of this flame, we can go forth into the world as a beacon of warmth and light.

Positive Fire Qualities ★ Warm, enthusiastic, spirited, idealistic, honest, exuberant, playful, self-motivated, sincere, action-orientated, self-expressive, open, generous, romantic, illuminating, direct, freedom-seeking, optimistic, future-orientated, self-confident, passionate, creative, individualistic, spontaneous, generous, adventurous, pioneering, initiating, inspiring, spiritual, visionary. Fiery temperaments are positive and extroverted, pushing ahead through life with charisma, confidence and buoyancy. They are demonstrative, dramatic, intense and affectionate, with a strong intuitive quality.

Negative Fire Qualities ★ Self-centred, impatient, unrestrained, without boundaries, pushy, careless, reckless, overconfident, insensitive, wilful, self-deluding, volatile, childish, unable or unwilling to reflect, sulky, lacking in perspective, hasty, angry, impractical, thoughtless, forceful, intrusive, restless, immature, driven by desires and sexual urges, egocentric, extravagant, overbearing, melodramatic, imposing, tactless, comes on too strong, temperamental, ungrounded, wild, hyperactive, impulsive, unstable, inconsistent, clumsy, out of touch with own body, and explosive. Fiery temperaments can suffer from 'burnout' through their excessive enthusiasm, energy and impulsivity, and may feel flat or depressed when life deals them a blow.

THE ARCHANGEL OF FIRE ★ MICHAEL

An archangel is an angel of greater than ordinary rank. They possess a stronger, more powerful essence than the guardian angels, through overseeing and guiding the other angels who are said to be with us here on Earth. The word 'angel' derives from the Greek word *angelos* meaning 'messenger'. To humans, angels are often seen as bringers as all sorts of messages. Angels in all their forms are believed to bring the message of 'spirit' into matter, carrying the blueprints of creation and the Source from the Divine into the manifest world. Angels are not and never have been human; they, like fairies and nature spirits, are part of a different evolutionary pattern – but they do appear to us in human form (usually with wings) because that is what we understand. An angel can be in many different places at once, and with the same intensity and concentration, and wish for us to be aware of them and benefit from them.

There are said to be three categories of angels in the cosmos, each with three subdivisions *. 'Angel' is the generic term and also relates specifically to those closest to the physical. Similarly, archangel may be taken to mean any of the higher orders, and indeed signifies the order just above ordinary 'angel'. Found in a number of religious traditions, the word 'archangel' itself is usually associated with the Abrahamic religions. The word archangel is of Greek origin, and means literally 'chief angel'. All archangels end with the 'el' suffix, 'el' meaning 'in God' and the first part of the name meaning what each individual Angel specialises in. The archangel who rules your sign will be the one with whom you most resonate. The astrological sign is an energy signature, a matrix of a specific stellar pattern that will subtly affect and influence you. Although there are many associations for the great archangels of the Universe, we must keep in mind there is great overlapping in their duties and guidance. For example, we may say that one is for healing and another for protection, but they can all perform the functions of the others, and each has only areas of greater focus and responsibilities. Four of the multitude of archangelic beings work intimately with the Earth. These are Raphael (Air), Michael (Fire), Gabriel (Water) and Uriel (Earth). Associated with each of these archangels are one of the four elements, specific colours, one of the four directions or quarters of the Earth, three signs of the zodiac, and a variety of other energies and powers. Understanding these associations and considering them in relation to our own paths, can help us determine with which of them we are more likely to resonate. Your sign, being of the Fire element, vibrates to the essence of Michael.

* The first sphere, the *Heavenly Counsellors*, comprises Seraphim, Cherubim and Thrones. The second sphere, the *Heavenly Governors*, comprises Dominions, Virtues and Powers. The third sphere, the *Heavenly Messengers*, comprises Principalities, Archangels and Angels. Of course, all such classifications are a human construct, a way of placing order upon the unknowable and allowing us to perceive something about which we have no words to express. However, as long as we think of angelic hierarchies as a way of working with celestials, of remembering important attributes, and we are able to imagine and experience these beings, this order of angels will prove useful to those wishing to draw upon their messages and assistance.

★ ARCHANGEL MICHAEL'S ASSOCIATIONS ★

Element of Fire
The southern quarter of the Earth
The Autumn season
The colour red
The astrological signs of Aries, Leo and Sagittarius

Michael, meaning "Who is like God or the Divine," is the leader of all the archangels and is in charge of courage, truth, strength and integrity. He protects us physically, emotionally and psychically. Michael helps us to follow our truth without compromising our integrity, and helps us find our true natures so we can be faithful to who we really are. Overall, Michael is the archangel of protection, peace, safety, clarity, balance, and moving forward. This being works to bring patience and a safeguard against any psychic imbalances or dangers. Michael helps us to tear down the old and build the new.

LEO'S ZODIAC ARCHANGEL ★ MICHAEL

Additionally, each sign is associated with a particular archangel. Such knowledge can help you to build up a relationship with these beings, based upon your strengths and needs. However, no link is rigid, and as you work with angels you will come to develop your own affinities. When invoking a specific archangel, a useful ritual to draw them closer is to light a candle in that angel's colour, burn some oil or incense of its scent, and hold the appropriate crystal while focusing on what you are needing guidance on.

YOUR ARCHANGEL ★ Please see previous information under the heading 'Archangel Michael's Associations'.

SCENT/OIL ★ Frankincense

CANDLE COLOUR ★ Bright yellow, sapphire blue

CRYSTAL ★ Amber, topaz and sapphire

THE DEVIC REALMS & FIRE ★ SOUTH: REALM OF THE SALAMANDERS

"Through magick we do conjure the Elements, evoking unto us the special properties of the Lifeforce for our learning and our coming-into-light. And yet are there secret paths of knowledge that have fallen from the minds of men ... For the way of Magick is a path to sacred knowledge, of reverence and humility - and the world is a wondrous place. Yet how many amongst us have fathomed these depths?"
***Merlin's Book of Magick and Enchantment*, Nevill Drury**

Deva is a Sanskrit word that means 'shining one'. Devas are the life force within nature, and there are four devic realms - Fire, Earth, Air and Water - which contain ethereal elemental spirits or sprites. Elementals are the building blocks of nature, and close to being true energy and consciousness. The four elements correspond to four different states of matter: energy/transmutation (Fire), gas (Air), liquid (Water) and solid (Earth), which are linked to the four human states of consciousness: inspiration, thought, feeling and practicality. There are four spirits, or elementals, which reside in the devic realms, associated with each element. People have been painting pictures, telling stories and writing about these devic realms for hundreds of years, albeit sometimes through disguised mediums such as fairy tales or children's fantasy stories like Tolkien's *Lord of the Rings*. The power of the natural world is easily observed and since ancient times primal forces have been ascribed to various spirit beings. Belief in nature spirits is of such ancient origin and is Universal; cultures everywhere have names or words to describe them. In the sixteenth century, a famous Swiss physician, alchemist and mystic called Paracelsus * defined these beings as 'Elementals', classifying them according to the element of nature they inhabit. There are four main levels of elemental beings: Gnomes (Earth), Undines (Water), Sylphs (Air), and Salamanders (Fire). The fifth element of Ether is the element from which came forth the other four, and Ether, or Spirit, has never been defined in any particular category, and encompasses the aspects and beings of all the other elements.

Elementals are usually benevolent guardian beings or spirits that look after nature's secrets and treasures in whatever part of the natural realm they occupy. They can only be seen or 'felt' by those possessing heightened psychic abilities, yet they can be summoned by those practising alchemy, spells and magic in order to harness the forces of nature for their own particular intentions. In our modern lives, it may seem as though this magic doesn't exist, but the truth is that most of us are simply less in touch with it than ever before. The consequence of this is that we are destroying vast areas of land, polluting waters, creating toxic landscapes, and disrespecting the laws of nature, which often whisper their messages softly. It is therefore important for us to look at the beauty that surrounds us with true appreciation and genuine regard, and to open ourselves up to the magic resides within it. The four devic realms can teach us much about nature; they act as custodians for the four elements, and learning to work with them is a way of attuning to all the energies and beings of nature. Elementals are four-dimensional, and have nothing to obstruct their movements. Therefore, they move as easily through matter as we do through air and space. They do require some contact with humans for their own evolution. Helping to direct them is an overseer, traditionally called the King of that element, and an archangel. Each of these elements is affiliated with one of the four directions and each elemental spirit embodies its own special energy. If you wish to re-connect and re-harmonise yourself by working with nature and its messages and lessons, you could begin by learning a little about your element's realm: Your element is Fire, which is connected with the South direction and the realm of the Salamanders.

* Paracelsus is considered the most original medical thinker of the sixteenth century. His belief in supernatural beings, intuition and the invisible causes of illness helped him discover hydrogen and nitrogen. Paracelsus believed that "Elementals are unlike pure spirits for they are mortal, but they are not like man for they have no soul."

★ SALAMANDERS ★

These are not to be confused with the reptile salamanders, although they have the same name. Fire spirits are described as thick, red and dry-skinned beings called salamanders, which look similar to the common scaleless lizard-like amphibians that share their name. Elemental salamanders are sometimes visible as small balls of fire and have also been seen in the shape of tongues of flame that can run over fields and peer into dwellings. No fire is lit without their help. In fact, the salamander comes from the Greek word *salambe*, meaning 'fireplace'. These spirits control all manner of flame, lightning, explosions, volcanoes and combustion. Mostly they are active underground and internally within the body and mind. Salamanders evoke powerful emotional currents in humans, and stimulate fires of spiritual idealism and perception. Their energy is much like that of the Tarot Card, The Tower, assisting in the tearing down of the old and the building of the new - as fire can be both constructive and destructive in its creative expression.

The salamanders are the guardians of summer and Fire, and reside in the realm of passion, change, prophetic visions, personal power, inspiration and the inner child. They function in the physical body by aiding circulation and in maintaining proper body temperature, and working with the body's metabolism for greater health.

Fire elementals work with humans via heat, fire and flame. This includes everything from the flame of a candle to the ethereal flames and daily light of the Sun. They can be powerfully effective in healing work, but must be used carefully for such applications, as their energies are dynamic and difficult to control. They are almost always present when there is any healing going to occur. Fire provides us with warmth, fuel and heating, and voraciously destroys the old so new life can spring forth out of the ashes - it is the essence from which the legendary phoenix arises. Fire also represents the inner child, that place of innocence from which we all stem. As it gives rise to sexual fervour it is also the root of our creative spirits. The fire elementals can indeed awaken in us higher spiritual visions and aspirations. They strengthen and stimulate the entire auric field to enable easier attunement to and recognition of Divine forces within our lives.

The salamanders can be seen in the heart of fires, dancing like dragons in the flames, and this dragon symbology is used in many Eastern religions to pay homage to them. Salamanders love the Fire for it is nourished by it - yet it is so cold within itself that it cannot be harmed by the flames. They help blacksmiths in their task of forging mighty swords and armour, feeding strength into the flames to have it then yield into the blacksmith's purpose. And yet the salamander is a mighty and tenacious defender of Fire. Only the strongest powers can hold it at bay - it can then be a loyal ally and not an enemy to bar us on our quest. The King of Fire is Belenos or Djin, its archangel is Michael, its magickal tool is the wand (which calls down the spirits into form), and its sacred ceremonial stones are Yellow Topaz, Amber and Citrine.

INVOKING THE FIRE DEVAS

If you wish to increase your sexual prowess, inspiration or creativity, need some career or goal luck, are fearful of an imminent but necessary change or move, or you are in need of courage or energy to meet a challenge, ask the fire devas for their help.

You can encounter salamanders most easily in a bonfire or open hearth. Some see them as sparks or flashes of colour. Dragon-like beings that live within flames, you can see them coiling within the swirling and lapping heat of the flames, and watch others dance and crackle in the sparks. They also reside in every beam of sunlight and flow of electricity. If you do not have access to a proper fire, a candle can serve the same purpose: call upon their help by meditating upon a lit candle. Lighting several at once, particularly in the colours of red and orange, may heighten the power.

THE SOUTH DIRECTION'S CORRESPONDENCES

If you wish to work more with your particular element and direction, the following may help propel your wishes and magical journey:

Time of Day ★ Noon
Polarity ★ Male, negative
Exhortation ★ To dare
Musical Instruments ★ Brass instruments
Colours ★ Scarlet red
Season ★ Summer
Magical Instrument ★ Sword, dagger, athame
Altar Symbol ★ Lamp
Communion Symbol ★ Heat
Archangel ★ Michael
Human Sense ★ Sight
Art Forms ★ Dance, drama
Animals ★ Salamanders, lizards

Mythical Beast ★ Dragon
Magical Arts ★ Ritual
Guide Forms ★ Sun, protector god
Meditation ★ Bonfires
Images & Themes ★ Flames, volcanoes, midday Sun, walking through fire

HOW YOU CAN GET IN TOUCH WITH YOUR FIRE ENERGY

"To be alive is to be burning"

★ Use Fire energy when making wishes around the following: Banishing bad habits, enthusiasm, initiative, inspiration, playfulness, leadership, bringing out the inner child, courage, confidence, dynamic energy, psychic protection, passion and desire

★ In magical practices, Fire can be represented by a candle (red or yellow will strengthen its fiery association), a fireplace, smudge sticks, bonfires or, symbolically, a wand. The candle wax of a burning candle represents Fire's powers of change and transformation - melting as it burns, changing its shape and substance

★ The best days on which to employ Fire magic are Tuesday, ruled by the fiery red planet Mars, or a Sunday, ruled by the blazing Sun. If possible, choose midday when the Sun is at its zenith

★ Eat spicy, hot foods, such as chilli and cayenne, and use fiery spices and sauces

★ Burn a bridge, clean a slate

★ Write your wish/es down on a piece of red paper, then burn it to release the smoke along with its message into the Universe to be fulfilled

★ Spend time in the Sun every day if possible, and around fires of all kinds - stoves, candles, fireplaces, camp fires

★ Yellow and orange-coloured crystals will activate your connection with the element of Fire and enhance your creativity.

★ Practice candle magic

★ Drink green tea

★ Indulge in forms of caffeine such as coffee and chocolate, but do so moderately or you may become jittery, scattered and jumpy, and therefore render your inner Fire ineffective

★ Use supplements which are designed to support and believed to enhance your Fire energy, such as ginger, spirulina and ginseng. Some energy bars may also prove beneficial

★ Practice deep breathing and meditation exercises and disciplines, which help to increase and circulate energy and blood throughout your body

★ Meditate using the Fire mantra "Ram"

★ Indulge in sexual release regularly

★ Schedule and maintain an ongoing physical exercise routine

★ Learn and practice yoga

★ Create a 'Fire ritual', during which you regularly 'burn' away something which needs releasing or banishing

★ Take an acting, drama or theatrics class - or better still, become an actor on camera or on stage!

★ Learn about Fire gods and goddesses, and how they can benefit you. The Hawaiian Fire goddess Pele, is a great place to start

★ Meditate on the Wands suit in the Tarot (the Wands suit represents the Fire element)

★ Express yourself regularly and freely, either through the expressive arts, social events, or even a journal

★ Be bold, brave and courageous, even when you are not feeling like it

★ Choose a challenge and rise to it

★ Build your confidence daily by listing three achievements or goals you have reached, no matter how seemingly small or large

★ Wear and surround yourself with the colours red and orange

★ Commit yourself to a bright future by creating a vision or dream, and maintain it by keeping track of your steps along the way

★ Think and act big. As Marianne Williamson said: "Our deepest fear is not that we are inadequate. Our deepest fear is that we are powerful beyond measure. It is our light, not our darkness, that most frightens us. Your playing small does not serve the world ... We are all meant to shine as children do ... And as we let our own lights shine, we unconsciously give other people permission to do the same." So be bold and shine!

★ When working with the Fire element in magical practice, stand at the South quarter of your magical space, as the South is its domain, and invite its living essence into your circle or space

★ Fire spirits are known by metaphysicians as salamanders, and they inspire passion, blessings, new life, creativity, and spiritual healing. With all this in mind, Fire signs would be wise to adopt one as their very own spirit guide!

YOUR MODE ★ FIXED

> "Leo embodies the quality of fixity with the element of fire. This means that Leo is the eternal flame"
> **Alan Oken, Astrologer & Author,**
> *As Above So Below*

Each sign belongs to one of the three quadruplicities, Cardinal, Fixed and Mutable. If we closely examine the Earth's yearly cycle, we can form a very accurate picture of the nature of these quadruplicities, for they correspond directly with the manifestation of the seasons. Each season has three months: the first month brings the new phase of the cycle, the second month brings a concentration of the season's energy to its fullest expression, and the third month represents the transition from the current season to the next one. The astrological quadruplicities represent the three basic qualities in all life: creation (Cardinal), perseveration (Fixed) and destruction (Mutable). Every thing that is born, from a period of time to a human being, experiences a life and then dies. In this context, death can be taken to mean that the form of the energy changes; but the energy itself can never be annihilated, for form is mortal, whereas essence is immortal.

The Fixed mode covers the signs Taurus, Leo, Scorpio and Aquarius, and is the most determined and unshakable of the three qualities. The positive side of the Fixed signs is stability. You are the builders, whether of Earthly creations (Taurus), artistic endeavours (Leo), occult powers (Scorpio), or world-changing visions and ideas (Aquarius).

The Fixed mode signifies the manifestation of purpose and its subjects are concerned with ownership, concentration, stability, fixation, and working with a cool head and calm demeanour under pressure.

The Fixed quality is associated with stabilisation, depth, preservation, persistence, loyalty and strength of will. You operate with purpose, dedication, self-reliance and determination, happy to forge ahead, through calmly working away, until you have achieved your ultimate goals. Fixed signs are a fearsome, formidable and quietly forceful group, able to follow their will and demonstrate fixity, often to the point of being stubborn, win-at-all-costs and wilful. Rarely are you distracted in your quests, for you have the ability to stay on firm course and track until a project's end. You are enduring, deliberate, steady and stable, but may be rigid and single-minded. You have a strong sense of routine, ritual and control. You work hard to consolidate and preserve the things that matter to you, but you can also be inflexible and resistant to change. You stick with situations even when they are outworn, uphold the status quo, and are loyal and dependable, but hate to give in and may lack spontaneity. Your energy and nature is powerful, robust, concrete, limited, set in its ways, purposeful, conscientious, slow, consistent, enduring, stubborn, innately cautious, rigid, unimpulsive, opinionated, unchanging, and you are generally strong in opinions, habits, likes and dislikes. Not easily distracted, you always keep your eyes on the prize, but you have a tendency to brood or to become stuck in a rut. You also project an image of strength as an effective shield against your considerable vulnerability. The Fixed mode indicates the midpoints of the seasons, which are very strong ritualistic times and 'fixed points', signifying points of power in the zodiac. Because Fixed signs fall in the middle of the season, this term signifies that the season is firmly established - fixed - by the time the Sun enters these signs.

Leo is the most vibrant and showy of the Fixed signs, and has the highest fondness and aptitude for power, prestige and creativity.

YOUR RULING PLANET ★ THE SUN

Your True Essential Core Self

Planetary Meditation
I am my Earth (my body),
and my Sky (my transcendence)
I am my Sun (my spirit),
and my Moon (my soul)
I am my Venus (my pleasure),
and my Jupiter (my faith)
I am my Mars (my courage),
and my Saturn (my lessons)
I am my Mercury (my thoughts),
and my Uranus (my truth)
I am my Neptune (my dreams),
and my Pluto (my transformation)

Each planet has its own distinctive and original meaning which, according to its position in the zodiac, combines with the qualities that are inherent in each of the twelve astrological signs. If a planet is your sign's ruler, however, it exerts a significant influence upon your life, regardless of its birth chart or zodiacal position.

> The Sun whose rays are all ablaze
> with every-living glory
> Does not deny his majesty;
> he scorns to tell a story
> He doesn't exclaim, 'I blush for shame,
> so kindly be indulgent',
> But fierce and bold in fiery gold

he glories all effulgent.
I mean to rule the Earth as he the sky.
We really know our worth, the Sun and I.
Unknown

Luminary ★ Associated with the Authentic Self, Essence, Identity, Ego, Creativity, Life Force, Will, Spirit, Purpose ★ 365 Day Cycle

★ KEY WORDS ★

Self-Expression, Vitality, Creativity, Identity, Centre, Core Self, Majesty, Inner Guiding Light, Source, Essence, Authentic Self, Pride, Life Force, Power, Purpose, Will, Potential, Talents, Assertiveness, Honour, Self-Confidence, the Masculine Self, Leadership, Determination, Authority, the Father, Consciousness, Awareness, Ambition, the Present, Spirit

★ KEY CONCEPTS ★

★ The Individual ★ Outlook on Life ★
★ The Indestructible Self ★
★ The Father ★ Success and Achievement ★
★ The Masculine Expression ★
★ Consciousness ★
★ Glamour and Glitter ★
★ Self-integration ★
★ The Creative Principle ★
★ The Animating Force of All Life ★
★ Electricity ★
★ Nucleus of the Atom ★
★ Vitality of the Organism ★

Day ★ Sunday

Number ★ 1

Basic Energy & Magic ★ Will, Success

Colours ★ Gold, Orange, Deep Yellow
Gods/Goddesses/Angel ★ Helios, Sol, Michael

Metal ★ Gold, Brass

Gems/Minerals ★ Diamond, Amber, Citrine, Topaz

Trees/Shrubs ★ Juniper, Laurel, Palm

Flowers/Herbs ★ Marigold, Saffron, Sunflowers, Cinnamon, Peony, Musk, Frankincense, Yellow Poppy, Chamomile, Mistletoe, Almond, Heliotrope

Wood ★ Walnut

Animal ★ Lion, Hawk

Element ★ Fire

Zodiacal Influences ★ Rules Leo; Exalted in Aries; Detriment Aquarius; Fall Libra

The Sun occupies a unique position in astrology. Unrivalled by any other planetary body, it stands out, towering above the rest by virtue of the fact that all the planets revolve around *it*. It is the main attraction, the leader of the pack. The Sun has always been symbolic of our directed will and sense of purpose; a strong Sun in a horoscope correlates with a strong sense of purpose. The Sun, as the giver and sustainer of all life, is a vast and unconquerable life-force.

The Sun, is, quite simply, our true essential conscious self. It is our authentic, pure *be*-ing, as it is not veiled by superficialities or accumulated emotions. Indeed, tear these down and you are left with your Sun. Our Sun is our personal powerhouse, our genuine self, rather than that which is filtered through façades, masks, boundaries, fears and external conditioning. Before we 'become' our Sun however, it is the energy that holds together the disparate parts of the self until these can be integrated as we develop and mature.

The Sun is not a planet but a star. In astrology, it is referred to as a planet for clarity purposes. But considering that the origin of the word 'planet' is a Greek term that translates as 'wandering star', perhaps this is not so far off the mark after all.

The Sun is the generator of life, the channel through which our self-expression is expressed outward, and the motivating force behind all activities. Like the physical heart, its energy operates and emanates from our centre, our *core*. The Sun is an energising, enlightening giver of life and vitality. It reveals much about the type and amount of energy available to us, and also how we use it to propel ourselves through life. Representing the spirit, it reveals our creative abilities as well as our general overall health, strength and fervour. Harmony between one's outer world and one's Solar purpose is perhaps the best indicator of good, sound overall health.

Often regarded as a 'fixed star', this is true of the Sun only in the sense that it is the point in the vastness of space around which the Earth and other planets revolve. Historically, the Sun is the chief and central deity of all cultures. Over time, it became representative of the Solar System's God-principle. To the Hindus the Sun was known as Brahma; it was Mithra to the Persians, Lugh to the Celtics, Bel to the Chaldeans, Hu to the Druids, Amun-Ra and Aton to the Egyptians, Apollo to the Romans, Helios to the Greeks, and Sol to the Latins. The Hebrew word for Sun is *Ashahed*, meaning 'all-bountiful fire'.

Since we live in a Solar ecology, we already know a great deal about how the Sun works and its power in our lives. Essentially a star, this mass is 1,300,000 times the size of Earth and about 750 times the combined mass of all other bodies in its system. What we see when we look at the Sun through a photographic filter, is not a solid object but a sphere of gas burning at about 6,000 degrees Celsius on the surface and reaching temperatures of 20,000,000 at the centre. The Solar centre, or 'nucleus', though in a gaseous state, is extremely dense, nine times the density of iron. With all this in mind, it is easy to imagine why the Sun is the unrivalled mighty ruler of our collective existence, and indeed, of our individual natal birth charts. Furthermore, it is the closest thing to immortality we can perceive in our world, with a future lifespan that seems beyond even the power of the human imagination. However, it is well to keep in mind that the Sun is only such a phenomenal concept because of our perspective of it from Earth. In reality, it is probably one of the feeblest and tiniest stars in the entire Universe. This star, from which we receive our energy vibrations, is certainly not stable. Astronomers tell us it is nothing but a ball of gases, constantly devouring and rekindling itself, held together solely by the regenerative force of its own combustion. Additionally, photographs show that it fluctuates in size, emitting sudden flashes out into the void, and then folding back upon itself - in essence, experiencing constant deaths and subsequent rebirths.

Nonetheless, from our standpoint here on Earth, astrologers are not wrong in agreeing that the Sun sign is the focal point of any astrological birth chart in the same way that it is the focal point of our physical existence, wellbeing and survival. As the heavenly body which shines the brightest, an astrologer will invariably check one's Sun placement in a birth chart first, for it reveals intriguing clues as to where an individual will shine at their optimum fullest in life. Although fundamentally human beings do not differ globally in many ways, every one of us knows our self as an individual. We feel in our spirits, our minds, our physical bodies, a sense of personal identity. Each of us knows our self to be unique and in a large sense we are. It is this concept of selfhood, this ability to say, "I Am," which astrology attributes to the Sun force.

In ancient times, the alchemical Sun frequently stood as a metaphor for sulphur, a fiery, burning substance. In psychological terms, 'sun' or 'sulphur' or the 'Solar lion' signified the vital commanding life-force, that same force which manifests itself in our daily lives as the ego. The Sun or inner king is for most of us what it was to those old cultures - the vital force and masculine directive principle. According to the alchemists, the Self can only appear when the king unites with the queen in a mystical or sacred union, of Sol and Luna, the Sun and Moon. They asserted that the true emergence of the Self is dependent upon this marriage of masculine and feminine qualities within the human psyche.

Traditionally, the Sun is in fall in Libra, which is the symbolic 'sunset point' in the astrological mandala. Here the individual's will and purpose is suppressed somewhat by the desire to compromise or harmonise with others. And though the Sun is considered weak in its expression when in Libra, its symbolism reveals one thing that the Solar ego is not good at: *relating*. The Sun is essentially a self-centred, egocentric power, driven by an individual's own self-satisfying desires. Strongly Solar people are therefore considered to be self-absorbed, their sense of direction and achieving goals meaning everything to them. After all, they don't really have the inclination to relate to others and see others' viewpoints, as they are too busily involved in the business of leading and conquering the world. There is certainly an arrogance and self-interest in excessively Solar types, but bearing in mind the physical mechanics of our Solar system, it is also important to recognise that the planets *do* revolve around the Sun.

Just as the Sun is the centre of our galaxy, it is the energy centre of your birth chart; without the Sun, a horoscope would have no vitality, no colour.

The glyph (or symbol) for the Sun ☉ depicts a circle with a dot or 'seed' at its centre, from which the core self, power, creativity and the first sparks of life can spring, and representing the spirit's unlimited potential brought into focus. It signifies the emanation of light, and could be considered as the life-giving energy from the unlimited resources of the Divine. The circle around this 'seed', is a symbol for infinity, a perfect shape that is without beginning or end, representing spirit, symbolising wholeness, eternity and the never-ending flow of energy.

It is the Sun's inexhaustible light which vitalises all the other planetary bodies, for without its electromagnetic radiation there could be no life anywhere, either in the Solar system or in the human organism.

The Sun is commonly known as the great 'Father' of the zodiac, represents the father or father figure (an individual's experience and expectations of their father or father figure), how we express and experience our masculine side, and the male principle, indicating how strongly these manifest in an individual, whether female or male. The Sun describes how well the active, masculine component of the personality can flow. This energy comprises the psyche of both genders, and complements the flow of feminine energy. Symbolising the father, either as a parent, authority figure or other significant male influences, the Sun reveals our expectations and attitudes around our own father, as well as fathering itself.

Just as the Sun is the centre of our galaxy and by far our most important star, it is the energy centre of a birth chart. Without Solar power, planet Earth and all life upon it could not thrive or even survive, and likewise without the Sun our horoscope would have no life force or vitality. The Sun is found in the outer edges of the Milky Way galaxy and is the Earth's primary source of energy, warmth, sustenance and light. All nine known planets and their Moons in our Solar system revolve around the Sun (although when astrology first began, the prevailing worldview was that the planets revolved around the Earth). All the personal planets - that is the Moon, Mercury, Venus and Mars - as well as the two social planets Jupiter and Saturn, are the means through which the Sun works in developing one's true, authentic, core identity. Because of the Sun's importance, it is almost always the first and arguably the most significant, consideration in the interpretation of a natal chart. The Sun's qualities are waiting to be utilised and some basic astrological knowledge around its function can help strengthen the psyche's urge to expand by introducing individuals to their Sun's potential.

Ultimately, the Sun represents the search for - and indeed the need to be - one's *self*.

Being prominent as your ruling planet, the Sun's energy is manifested in the Lion's spirit through dramatic self-expression, inspired creativity and natural leadership. The Sun symbolises the natural radiance of your inner spirit. By embracing authoritative roles or creative outlets, you honour the Sun's energy. Negatively speaking, the Sun as your ruling planet can create excessive pride, an unreasonable need for attention and praise, or a desire to outshine others.

Our Sun (or star) sign refers to the constellation that the Sun falls in on our birthday. In a natal chart the Sun describes your personality, talents, spirit, ego, individuality, temperament, ambitions, drive, self-confidence, sense of self-worth, the ability to be self-sufficient, and our overall outlook on life. The placement of the Sun also indicates leadership qualities, the degree of desire for power and authority, willpower, strength, determination, resilience, the ability to conquer goals, and one's sense of pride and honour, as well as honours bestowed upon one. The Sun also shows us our playful, experimental and creative urges, the ability to bring new ideas and forms into existence, our capacity for pleasure, joy and happiness, and of course health, specifically our vigour, strength, energy levels, constitution and recuperative powers.

The Sun's function is to illuminate, vitalise, improve, individualise, stabilise, integrate and elevate. It is the primary expression of the instinctive inner self, individuality, the unfolding of our personality, the core around which are structured all the elements of one's character, nature and essence. The instinctive inner self is all about how we act spontaneously without thinking, and what creates and generates feelings of affinity, attraction, indifference and aversion inside us.

The Sun represents our individuality, our ability to stand apart from the rest, our inner shining light that can never be dulled or snuffed out, for its essence and energy are eternal and pure, and energy can never be created or destroyed. Strong Sun subjects, such as Leos, want to shine. Competitive, successful and outstanding in their fields, these people seek out accolades, recognition and applaud, but also fun, play and amusement for their own sake. Of all the planetary influences, with the exception of Venus, this is the most likely to make one apt to mix business with pleasure.

Something which is often overlooked is that the Sun is also associated with successful business ventures, and it is the creative aspect of such enterprises which comes under the providence of the Sun. A business, especially a small one, is often the manifestation of someone's personal creative vision. It can be confidently asserted that if the Sun shines upon a business venture, it will be blessed and a success.

The Sun also rules anything which glistens, therefore jewellery, ornaments and adornments, especially those made from gold, comes under its auspice. Into this category also falls show business, glamorous clothes, flamboyant people, entertainment, and dazzling, star-studded events.

The Sun is externalising, and represents totality, infinity, and the striving towards and ultimate attainment of your optimal personal potential. Endowing us with our inherent creative potential and personal identity, it describes our urge to *create* and to *be*.

Our greatest luminary represents the *present*, which is arguably our greatest gift, because the present moment is all we ever truly have. The same could be said for the Sun - for stripped bare of our pretensions, masks and false bravado, the Sun is all that remains and all that ever will.

The Sun rules the heart and is therefore symbolically the centre of self. Indeed, the Sun *is* the heart and the most commanding presence in our birth chart; the mighty Ruler who governs, guards and maintains our core essence.

The Sun is associated with Leo, achievement, greatness, kings, princes, egotism, leaders, officials, emblems, importance, aristocrats, pride, eyes, galas, magnificence, palaces, coronation, light, managers, solariums, illumination, pinnacles, lavish, arrogance, monarchs, spotlight, ornate, valuables, nobility, glory, influence, show-offs, life, Sunday, authority, grandeur, bosses, honour, celebrity, splendour, centre, chief, status, circles, royalty, colours, nucleus, rulers, conceit, males, commanding, fame, gold, confidence, orange, ostentation, pomp, renown, ceremony, crowns, diamonds, emperor, eminence, father, government, heart, power, prestige, radiance, sunny, theatres, vanity, sunshine, warmth, superiors, willpower, thrones, supremacy and VIPs. I'm sure you get the idea!

It could be said that most people do not live up to the potential of their Sun, for most of us are only dimly aware of our pure, undiluted essence. If you were to be in complete harmony with your Sun (self), then you would be able to achieve a high level of authenticity and self-mastery. Throughout our lives, we help and are helped; we learn and we teach. By developing the potentialities of our Sun sign into a deeper understanding and appreciation of the world and others around us, we send a brighter illumination back to those who may be straining behind us, and a strong beam forward to light the way ahead. The Sun has no pretences and no masks; where the Sun is found, nothing can be hidden. It illuminates the way - towards our goals, life purpose and ultimate destinies.

The Sun of the Tarot deck - card 19 of the Major Arcana - contains a very positive image and meaning, heralding health, joy, exuberance, success, good fortune and vitality.

The Sun is what calls you to your greatness. It is your potential, the truth of who you are and the truth of who you can be. If you are willing to heed its call, you can rightly go forth to claim your unique and individual greatness. Bringing together and balancing all the qualities of an individual and all the components of one's personality, its potential is the peak of constructive maturity and ultimate self-fulfilment. Through its power, we can only enjoy each moment and then let it go, confident that we carry the Sun within ourselves as we move along the eternal, illuminated journey.

This Solar energy and influence, throughout your whole life, gives Leos the gifts of luminosity, benevolence, leadership, playfulness, nobility, magnanimity, generosity and an abundance of creative expression. Too much of this Solar energy can make one vain, indolent, domineering, extravagant, elf-centred, condescending, boastful, proud, bombastic, sulky, arrogant, overbearing, pompous and a spotlight-hogger. But the true Lion is really just an overgrown, exuberant, bounding kitten with a heart substantial enough to embrace many, and a strength that allows him to rule the kingdom and conquer the enemy; after all, your motto is "I Will," because deep down, you really *will*. How will *you* use your phenomenally powerful Solar influence?

YOUR HOUSE IN THE HOROSCOPE ★ THE FIFTH HOUSE

The fun-spirited Fifth House is all about leisure, holidays, romance, hobbies, recreation, sport and speculation. It is connected with creativity in the broadest sense, children as a creative act, and romance as a true expression of ourselves.

A house is one of the twelve sections dividing the terrestrial globe, viewed from a precise time and geographical place, into sectors from the poles to the horizon. The horoscope, or birth chart, is divided into these twelve sections called houses. Each house governs a different area or 'department' of life, such as relationships, career, leisure and even karma. The reason for this division of the Earth into houses can be understood when we consider that the Sun's rays affect us differently in the morning, at noon and at night, and also in summer and winter, and if we study the cause, we will readily observe that it is the angle at which the ray strikes us or the Earth which produces that difference in effect. Similarly, with the stellar rays, astrologers have observed that a child born at or near midday, when the Sun's rays strike the birthplace from the Tenth House, has an improved chance of public or career advancement in life than one born after sunset. By similar observations and tabulations, it has been found that the other planetary rays affect the various departments of life when their ray is projected through the other houses, and therefore each house is said to 'rule' or govern certain departments of the human life experience.

The Fifth House, ruled by Leo, is the house of creativity, romance, children, love affairs, sex, games and gambling, amusements, and creative expression in all its forms. Recreation and leisure activities that are enjoyable and life-enhancing to the individual will be shown here; this house is where you play, develop a sense of wonder, and discover and express your inner child. Under these umbrellas fall things such as entertainment, holidays, vital energy, pleasures, the ability to love and procreate, and the relationship with one's offspring. Encompassing everything that is creative and artistic, including dreams, ideas, music, art and dancing, this is where the spirit goes forth in the world, where the inner landscape is made visible and tangible in the outside world.

It also reveals your level of originality and initiative, and the amount of love you are prepared to offer, including within courtship and lovemaking. It may even be said that the love referred to by this sphere is based on desire, passions and impulses, and that it is the particular and original expression of this desire within each one of us, which is the basis of our feelings and not the reverse. Other exoteric and esoteric keywords for the Fifth House include: Procreation, hobbies, games and sports, self-fulfilment, joy and bliss. If there is a strong sign or planets within this house, any or all of these will play a key role in your overall enjoyment of life.

Traditionally, the Fifth House is primarily concerned with creative self-expression. This can include artistic and leisure pursuits that you are attracted to, sports and lovers, or it could be those procreational instincts that lead to pregnancy, the production of children and then your relationship with them. Love, romance, your romantic life, sexual desire, dating and socialising not involving a deeper commitment, all come under the reign of the Fifth House also, but this is not the deep, serious, committed love of the Seventh House; rather it is the fun, playful kind of romantic love that is enjoyed for its pleasures and pure, uncomplicated simplicity.

The Fifth House marks the beginning of the journey of our individuality and our individual quest. At the first level, it concerns amusement, our sense of humour, how we approach play, and our play style. Level two deals with recognising the power of creativity and its impact on our social relationships and connections. At the third and highest level, the Fifth House deals with our integration of self-expression and the development and acquisition of a solid, secure ego strength.

The Fifth House broadly governs two areas of life - pleasure and creation. Creation refers not only to the children we bring into the world, but artistic work also, the talent for living life to the full, and developing our optimum potential. But the single *core* task of this house is the development of ego strength. As it is concerned with courtship, affairs, emotional experiences, sweethearts and lovers, it can reveal how we first have our heart broken or stolen, our experience of it and our journey to recapture it.

Further, we each have our own unique style of loving. While the planet Venus in our birth chart reveals the expression and manifestations of an individual's emotions, motivations and feelings, it is the Fifth House that describes the context in which these will be shown, the appearance they will take and how the individual will experience these feelings in the reality of social and material life. But it also has the function of informing us about the love or feelings towards any children that we may have. Some astrologers claim that in examining this House in the natal chart, it is quite possible to even determine whether or not the individual will have, or desires to have, children. Realistically, other elements of the chart are significant in reaching any thoughts around this, but the Fifth House is the strongest indicator in the horoscope when it comes to fertility and offspring, and the subject's attitudes around both.

Commonly known as the sector of luck, it also rules gambling, risk-taking, and all forms of speculation such as lotteries, the Pools, lotto, casinos, racing, the stock market and any other activities where there is an element of chance involved. This house is significant for joys and happy events in life; it will give directions as to what entertains us, and gains or losses at play, when there are favourable or unfavourable planets in the house respectively.

It relates to many of the things we think of as constituents of The Good Life, such as parties, gatherings, openings, events, pampering, treats, amusement, holidays, relaxation, social life, luxuries, celebrations, banquets and dinner parties, movies, dancing, and artistic, creative, mystical, theatrical, dramatic or cultural pursuits.

YOUR OPPOSITE SIGN ★ AQUARIUS
WHAT YOU CAN LEARN FROM THE WATER BEARER

If we look at the zodiac, we can see that it can be broadly divided into two hemispheres, this division being based on the natural division of the year by the two equinoxes. Astrologers often refer to the first six signs, the hemisphere in which the day predominates (the days being longer in the spring and summer months), as the Personal Sphere of Experience, and the second six signs, the hemisphere in which nights are longer, as the Social Sphere of Experience. These two halves of the zodiac perfectly balance and complement each other, and each individual 'personal' zodiac sign has something to teach its directly opposite 'social' zodiac sign.

To generalise, the signs of the personal sphere tend to experience life through a type of self-projection and self-interest which is often socially uncomplicated, unsophisticated or naïve. Their objective is to learn greater social awareness and thereby integrate themselves with the larger, more Universal human collective. On the other hand, the signs of the social sphere are prone to experience life through the use of their more developed social consciousness. In essence, the personal signs (Aries, Taurus, Gemini, Cancer, Leo, Virgo) usually provide stimulation and new energy to their environment, while the social, more Universal signs (Libra, Scorpio, Sagittarius, Capricorn, Aquarius, Pisces) provide experience, opportunities for wider expression, and give a more broad-minded approach and perspective to their surroundings.

Each sign in a pair seeks and is attracted to the qualities of its complementary opposing sign. Leo seeks the social inclusiveness of Aquarius, while the Aquarius desires the sense of individuality, confidence and strength of purpose embodied by Leo. Leo dwells within the realm of the organisation and projection of individual ambitions and *personal* ideals and creativity, while Aquarius resides within the realm of the organisation and projection of social ambitions and *collective* ideals and contributions.

"The Leo-Aquarius polarity can result in perfect harmony, for a King's greatest function in life is to be the ablest servant of the people. Leo will succeed when his personal ambitions are integrally linked to a higher humanitarian purpose."
Alan Oken

Positive and Fixed, the balance of this polarity is between the artist and the scientist, the individual and the group, the strong-ego and the absent-ego, the autocrat and the democrat. Leo is self-centred and radiates self-confidence like the Sun generates warmth, while the pure Aquarian is only one cog in a vast operating system and is not motivated by self-interest or ambition. Leo can be an egotistical and arrogant dictator who may become oblivious to the existence of those 'beneath' him, unless they serve as exploitable followers. Aquarius looks after the rights of others he considers his 'brothers', ever upholding causes and personal ideals that work towards the benefit of all. The Leo can be so intent on furthering his individual ego-based creativity, that he can easily lose sight of other people; through over-emphasising his own needs, he tends to neglect others and as a result, disregard their input. To help overcome this undesirable trait, he can look towards the group-oriented approach of Aquarius for support.

Although the word 'opposite' conjures up feelings of separateness and differences, the astrological polarities should not be seen as two signs in conflict with each other - their positive expression is to create a natural balance and equilibrium. Each sign has something to learn from its opposite, but also has a contribution to make towards the other sign's more evolved expression. The Fifth (Leo) and the Eleventh (Aquarius) House polarity is concerned with *personal* creativity versus *group* creativity and contribution

The Fifth House is concerned with pure instincts, pleasure, sensual desires, romance and leisure, whilst the Eleventh House is about a kind of intellectual and spiritual sublimation of love - but the two differing spheres can complement each other. They can even be said to present us with two extreme expressions of love: love given as simple desire and pleasure, and love as a gift we are free to give. The Fifth House is where a person consolidates and expresses his individuality and outer identity through various leisurely and creative pleasures, whereas the eleventh house is a less personal, more widely varying expression of one's individuality - usually concerning the individual in the context of a group or the wider society. It indicates one's altruistic attitudes and activities, friendships, social connections and broad motivations and aspirations, while the opposing Fifth House is much more individually-centred and self-oriented.

The modern associations between Aquarius and Uranus has given Aquarius an oft exaggerated reputation for being rebellious, difficult, wayward, eccentric, perverse and unstable. And indeed, all of these negative traits and behaviours arise as extreme manifestations in individuals who have not yet found their centre - or their heart. This is Leo's domain, and from this very centre he can teach a lot to his Water Bearer friends. However, Aquarius has much to teach Leo about adventures in non-conformity. Lions are ever eager to please and as much as they hate to admit it, to fit in and be liked, admired and popular. The Aquarian spirit will shrug this off and move in the other direction, marching to the beat of a distant drummer, and to the tune of his own harmonica. In other words, he shuns conventionality and the stereotypical images that the vain Leo adheres to in order to win friends and influence people. The Lion is afraid of stepping out of the square in case he loses his audience, but the Water Bearer can teach him that this is a risk well worth taking.

Although the Sun is in detriment in the sign of Aquarius (being opposite Leo, which is ruled by the Sun), the Water Bearer will usually still manage to make his mark on the world, and in a much less showy way than the Lion.

Aquarius is primarily an impersonal and group-oriented sign, and operates according to thinking principles. It is concerned with the energies of the group rather than with the personal creative unfolding of the individual. Leo is individualistic and uninterested in the group; he seeks above all to become what he envisions as his own heroic potential. This is all very well, until your ego trips you up. Aquarius can teach you how to become more focused on the needs of a wider group of people and social issues. Aquarius knows that to achieve this, first you must relinquish the desire to dominate other people, and to stop concerning yourself primarily with being the King in every endeavour. In other words, you must strive to become their *equal*. This is no easy task for an individual quite used to not only getting his own way time and again through sheer force and will, but who is accustomed to praise, accolades and adoration everywhere he goes. On Aquarius's plane, everyone is on the same level - no one sits atop a throne, much less a pedestal; everyone is regarded as the one and the same. This may take the Leonine spirit some getting used to. But it is a lesson worth taking on, as Aquarius can teach you much about humility, modesty and humbleness.

Indeed, there is no room for grandiosity in the Aquarian realm. He can teach you how you can transform your intense self-pride into the will that will benefit the lot of all - and how to have fun doing it. What's more, he can guarantee that the pride you feel after uplifting *others* to their potential, is far more satisfying than any other brand.

The pivotal insights you can harness from your complementary opposite, may catapult you into a much more noble, though no less majestic, world of razzle-dazzle. Things look different here, but this is a profound lesson for the Lion to learn - to walk *amongst* your kingdom rather than ruling them from afar or from 'up there', as you are prone to do. When you walk amongst others as equals, as comes so naturally to Aquarius, you will play your part in assisting with the evolution and unfoldment of humanity in light of the bigger picture and plans of creation. In fact, if you adopt the Aquarian way of doing things, even on the odd occasion, you can be a powerful agent in accelerating the development of global evolution and revolution.

Aquarius is logical, consistent and principled; Leo is dramatic, spontaneous, intuitive and seeks myth rather than harsh truths. Aquarius believes the whole is more important than the parts which compose it, seeking and applying hard facts and logical concepts, and behaves with the benefit of the collective group in mind; Leo seeks joy, self-expression, spontaneity, the right to believe in magic and to bring fairy tales alive on life's vast stage. Aquarius, on the other hand, with its innately broader viewpoint, will promptly wipe out the individual if it runs too rampant in life's theatre.

The creative individual, intent on developing his own uniqueness and creative power (Leo), seeks to become aware of the larger human family of which he is a part, so that he may offer his creative gifts with an objective understanding of their value to others (Aquarius). Aquarius, being a group-conscious individual, is aware of the importance of the needs of others around him, and goes about improving the lot for everyone else first, and only then will he attend to himself. The Leo can learn from this noble characteristic, and learn from the Aquarian how to put the needs of others before his own self-serving needs. He will find that a surprising paradox will occur as a result: as a result of considering the group, others will soon begin to help *him* further *him*self more.

With your Sun in Leo, you are naturally concerned by appearances and seek prestigious situations from which you can benefit. You love to be admired, and are easily convinced that you are always right. Well of course you are, if you're the boss! Aquarius, on the other hand, is much less concerned with the self and 'appearances' to him is only a word in the dictionary. While you may show yourself to be totally devoted to your friends and loved ones, you are conditional: you only display your love and affections provided that in return they give you unconditional respect and appreciation. Being ambitious, extravagant and sometimes authoritarian and domineering, you can adopt a black and white, inflexible attitude, whilst not having as much courage and willpower as you would lead others to believe. In order to temper these characteristics, you can turn to your opposite Aquarius and glean wisdom in the arts of a more flexible temperament, tolerance, acceptance of others, understanding, and being able to operate effectively and selflessly within wider groups. It is imperative that you learn how to be less involved with yourself so that you can see things without the screen of your own ego obscuring them.

Overall, transcending your ego in order to achieve loftier heights is your biggest key to the

Kingdom of the Aquarian Utopia. If you swallow your Leonine pride and heed some of the Universal messages encapsulated in the Water Bearer's essence, you will begin to increase your circle, rejuvenate and enrich your own self, and ultimately help bring about the ever-unfolding revolution leading to greater enlightenment of all humanity. After all, we are now entering the Age of Aquarius!

WHAT THE WATER BEARER CAN ULTIMATELY TEACH THE LION

Release ★ Ego, self-serving activities, individual focus, selfishness, bossiness, arrogance, narrow vision, condescendence, pride, self-centredness, vanity, the need to show off and impress

Embrace ★ Humility, modesty, wider focus on others, unselfish feelings, solidarity with others, tolerance, brotherhood, cooperation, equality, objectivity, broader vision, independence, the cultivation of friendships

Aquarius is intellectual, abstract, inventive, friendly to all, brotherly, impersonal, detached, unemotional, freedom-loving, unattached, humanitarian, liberal, political, identifies with humanity, group or social causes, is non-conforming, rebellious, group-oriented, cooperative, tolerant, truth-seeking, promotes equality, and is attuned to Universal laws.

The Water Bearer teaches you that yours is a quest towards service to humankind. In learning this, you will experience a struggle between your own personal needs and a sense of dedication to others. However, you need to lay aside your personal needs for honour, authority, praise and prestige, and use your talents to serve the wider world. To evolve to your fullest potential, you need to be more free-thinking and innovative; to share your ideas with others; to use these ideas for the betterment of humanity; to exploit your self-confidence and innate talents by embracing a wider crowd of people and causes; to shine for all rather than just lighting up your own path; to become objective and detached; to channel collective powers wisely and remember that we are all part of the greater Uni-verse (literally meaning 'one song'); and above all, to simply give more of yourself to others.

MAGIC, DRAWING, ATTRACTION, SPELLS, RITUALS, WISHING & POWER

A Note on the Universe

Within each of us resides the merging of the Sun and the Moon, the dance of the constellations, the vibrations of the planets, and the vast microcosm and macrocosm of the entire *Universe*. Uni means 'one' and Verse means 'song'; therefore, the word Universe literally means 'One Song'. If you learn to tune yourself in, you can even hear it!

What is Magic?

Magic is a kind of special energy that is beyond description, and like most kinds of energy it has its own rules and ways of being manipulated. It remains an elusive term, and no definition has ever really found Universal acceptance. Attempts to separate it from superstition, religion and other-worldly phenomena on the one hand, and 'science' on the other, are ridden with difficulties. However slippery the term 'magic' might be, there is a general agreement that most of us wish for more of its presence in our lives and often fall short of achieving this wish.

Those performing spells, 'asking the Universe', wishing, praying, or undertaking rituals, are using this very special energy to draw things to them. Learning to manipulate energy in these ways is never hard (and shouldn't be), but it can be complex and does require knowledge, practice, creativity, patience and above all, imagination. Most of us use simple magic every day, whether by saying little prayers, making wishes, visualising, and exchanging - sending out and receiving - good, positive or hopeful vibes. When you understand that all the forces and magic you need are *within* you, and you learn to *believe* in that power, you are then able to make all manner of changes to your life and, most importantly, yourself.

Magic is an invisible force which connects and permeates everything. Every thought you have and every action you take, will affect the strength of this force, and can be influenced and directed towards a specific purpose by using certain means. The most important of these are your intentions, facing in the direction of your desired outcome, your will and your *belief* that it works. The more you want something to happen, and the clearer you can visualise the desired outcome, the stronger your will and feelings towards it will be, ensuring an avalanche of amazing people, events and circumstances will flow into your experiences, gathering speed, momentum and power as it nears your goal or dream.

The Universe (or whichever higher power you believe in) works for us and through us. Ideas are given to us but they must be carried out *through* us, in the form of asking or acting or performing a ritual or casting a specific spell. The Universe's abundance is your abundance, and it flows through your mind into manifestation. The Universe or Divine Being in which you believe, gives you the necessary ideas and clothes them with all that is needed to bring them into form when we ask *believing*.

Based on ancient human beliefs, systems and superstitions, declaring what you want and acting out your deepest desires can actually help to make things happen. Magical ideas include the notion that thought affects matter and that the trained imagination can alter the physical world, that all aspects of the Universe are interdependent and that we can discover connections and correspondences between everyday occurrences and cosmic, or Divine, energies. A miracle or a wish coming true can suggest something is going on that extends beyond the laws of nature, that something unseen has occurred; but just because we cannot see it or touch it, it doesn't mean it's not there. Magic exists, especially if you truly believe it does, but science is so far incapable of capturing its essence or the rationale behind it. Personally, I prefer to leave that task to the higher powers of the Universe.

To help your dreams come true and to use your inborn power to its full effect, you can employ boosters based on the special energies and qualities of your Sun sign. These 'boosters' are chosen to be in alignment with the purpose of a particular goal, and contain energies of their own which will enhance the strength of your spell, prayer, ritual or 'asking'. Specific magical energies can be invoked by carrying out a spell or ceremony using specific herbs or colours, or on a particular day of the week, according to either your Sun sign (to heighten the power of the asking), and/or that is in sympathy with that for which you are asking (I have included days of the week for other Sun signs and spell types).

Some materials and boosters you can use to increase the power, magic or energy in any area of your life include: candles, wish lists (written on an appropriate piece of paper written with a specially-chosen writing tool), symbols, affirmations, chants, incense, herbs and flowers, locations, colours, days of the week, elements, crystals and gemstones, animal symbols, charms, talismans, amulets, gods and goddesses, essential oils, planetary hours and your Solar totem animals. All are covered, some more briefly than others, for your very special Sun sign to radiate the energy to powerfully draw your wildest dreams towards you

Overall, it pays to remember that the Universe (or whatever higher power/s or force/s you happen to believe in) creates *through* you that to which you give your attention. What you contemplate becomes the law of your being, and through your pure unwavering belief, is eventually brought through to manifestation on the material plane. What you think about is entirely up to you. But just be mindful that whatever you think about the most becomes your dominant thought, then your main point of attraction, and is ultimately magnified until it becomes your reality or your experience. So choose your thoughts with care. And to quote Ralph Waldo Emerson, "Be careful what you set your heart upon, for it will surely be yours." I carry a copy of this beautiful prophecy in my purse as its words resonate so strongly with me. In other words, be mindful about what you're wishing for, for you will most probably get it, whether it's good or bad - magic, after all, doesn't discriminate. Just make your dominant thoughts good ones, and you will attract everything you set your heart and intentions upon. Good luck!

ASTROLOGY & MAGIC

"Everyone practices magic, whether they realise it or not, for magic is the art of attracting particular influences, events and situations within human life. Magic is a natural phenomenon because the Universe is reflexive, responding to human thoughts, aspirations and desires …"
David Fideler, *Jesus Christ, Sun of God*

Astrology is the most sublime of the occult * sciences, while at the same time it is one of the most practical for everyday application, for it divines the human soul itself. The cosmos, particularly the patterns that formed across it at the exact moment we were born, indicates the road along which our mental and spiritual endowments are likely to impel us, therefore enabling us to prepare in advance for life's battles, pitfalls, milestones, celebrations and of course to make the utmost of opportunities. Such is the magic of the human mind, that it can 'see' into the future and relive the past without having to be physically present in either, and when combined with astrological *knowing*, particularly the knowing that springs from understanding some of the dynamics of our natal chart, however basic, our inner - and outer - magic can be lifted to phenomenal heights.

In ancient times, not only was astrology the ardent study of the most learned and powerful minds, but among the masses of ordinary people its authority and guidance was accepted and followed without question. How this powerful knowledge was used was - and still is - up to the individual, but all who used it applied it to their perceived advantage.

As primitive humans observed the skies, no doubt they gradually realised that certain stars upon which their fate depended accompanied the seasons, or certain times of the year. They may also have reasoned that if governed their fate, they also governed their bodies, and it is therefore conceivable that the skies were associated with Divine influence. Certain celestial influences were believed to emanate from the thirty-six decans of the signs, and the mysterious but apparent effect that they exercised upon humans were thought to be due to a subtle ether shed by the heavenly stars and spheres on the Earth, that affected not only people, but also other animals, plants and minerals. For the ancient mind, linking magic with astrology may have also provided a much needed sense of predictability and patterns.

Early astrologers named and made associations with the imaginary divisions of the twelve signs and the twelve houses, and people born under a certain sign were said to inherit to an extent, its properties and nature. They also believed that the influence of the planets and stars corresponded with the medicinal properties of certain plants and minerals. They therefore asserted that the influence of a star or planetary position would affect the type of medicine or healing they would offer a subject to attain the most beneficial outcome. Throughout the writings of early philosophers and theorists, there is constant reference to this unmistakable mystic connection between the seven known planets and Earthly affairs and ailments. The seven metals were connected with the seven planets, to which the seven colours and the seven transformations were added. So the alchemist came to share the astrological doctrine that each planet ruled some mineral: The Sun ruled gold, the Moon silver, Mars iron, Venus copper, Saturn lead, Jupiter tin, and Mercury quicksilver. Consequently, in alchemical symbolism the same sign came to represent the metal and its corresponding planet.

In subsequent years, astrology became closely related to alchemical knowledge and development, and the alchemist came to be regarded as an authority not only on the transmutation of metals, but also on astrology and magic. This goes some of the way to explaining how magic and divination, which had always been inseparably bound up with astrology, came to be associated with alchemy. In all the occult sciences, the supreme power was believed to be in the stars above, and from their mysterious emanations all the metals, crystals, minerals, plants and herbs derived their special properties over time. Further, as alchemy became ever more spiritual and concerned with more abstract and philosophical concepts, eventually it was considered that the transmutation of lead into gold was simply a metaphor for the transformation of base matter, in this case the human soul, into a much purer and higher state of wisdom and being.

The Sun and Moon were believed to have greater influence over the human body than all the other heavenly bodies, and to exert their influence in various ways whenever they entered a certain sign of the zodiac. And although the Moon was traditionally regarded as the most important factor of a horoscope, the Sun has come into its own in later centuries, with the result that almost everyone knows their Sun sign but only those who have delved deeper are aware of the sign their natal Moon falls in. For this reason, I have chosen to focus this book series on the twelve Sun signs, as this is what the majority of people are most familiar with.

The following pages contain methods, energies, materials and objects which may be used to increase the magic and power of your Sun sign's influence upon you. Precious stones, flowers, colours and so on, are regarded as having a potent effect upon good fortune by attuning your mind to receive harmonious vibrations from the astral forces that surround you.

Finally, a basic working knowledge of basic astronomy and astrology is an asset when working with luck, abundance, wealth and personal power. You can attract more of these things when you align yourself with the workings of the wider Universe, the movement of the Sun, stars, Moon and planets and become aware of the correlations between the outer cycles of the skies and the inner cycles within yourself. Also, for those who are knowledgeable about Moon phases, equinoxes and solstices, a world of lucky possibilities can also magically open up to you. You don't need to know about astrology's deepest complexities to understand how everything interrelates; just learning the basics will give you an edge - and hopefully the following lucky tips will provide you with at least a small glimpse into the insights gleaned from your Sun sign, which I am certain will endow upon you the potential for amazing results to manifest in your life - and maybe even a step up one further rung towards the heavens!

* The word 'occult' comes from the Latin *occultus*, which literally means 'knowledge of the hidden'.

USING COLOURS, CRYSTALS, DEITIES, PLANTS, FOODS & MATERIAL SUBSTANCES FOR INCREASING POWER & MAGNETISING MAGIC

Alchemist, reformer and mystic Henry Cornelius Agrippa, born in 1486, in his principal work, *On Occult Philosophy*, expressed his belief in the doctrines of astrology and in the theory that the spirit of the world exists in the body of the world, just as the human spirit exists in the body of man. He contended that this spirit also abounds in the celestial bodies and descends in the rays of stars, so that the things influenced by their rays become conformable to them. By this spirit every occult property is conveyed into metals, stones, herbs and animals, through the Sun, Moon and planets, and even through the stars beyond and higher than the planets. A firm believer in the efficacy of charms, he stated that they may "be worn on the body bound to any part of it or hung around the neck, changing sickness into health or health into sickness." I believe the same effect could be applied to wishing and the thinking of positive thoughts, to mean, "Changing thoughts and dreams into manifest reality." He also recommended that these charms be worn in the form of finger rings (that have been created using the materials in agreement and harmony with your Sun Sign's magical energy).

Material substances are connected with abstract purposes by a complex but highly usable and accessible system of correspondences. Use these time-honoured connections in your own spells and wishes to magnetise your desires to you. The following pages will give you some materials, energies, forces and ideas you can summon the power of in order to enhance your magic and luck.

PLANETS

The Planetary influence of the day is important when 'asking' for something. If you are wishing for luck, for example, try working with your Sun sign's inherent energies combined with the perfect day of the week for it. So a Leo might try using his natural flair for articulate expression, to ask for greater luck on a Thursday, which is Jupiter's Day and Jupiter is renowned for being a lucky planet, or better still, ask for luck on a Sunday, which is the Sun's Day, ruler of Leo, at the time of day when Jupiter's influence is at its most powerful (information about planetary hours for each day of the week can be found on the Internet or in books on the subject, and can be complex and detailed. It is an art to memorise the correct times, days and energies for the correct spells. If you are determined enough to achieve your dream or goal however, you will be determined enough to put in the research to do it properly!) Here is a very simplified list of the days of the week and their meanings:

DAYS OF THE WEEK & THEIR POWERS

MONDAY ★ Moon
Cancer

The Divine feminine, changes, intuition, emotions, secrets, dealing with women, purity, goodness, perfection, unity, psychic ability, magic, spirituality, invoking a goddess's or angel's guidance, anything that fluctuates, contracts, increases or decreases.

TUESDAY ★ Mars
Aries & Scorpio

Enthusiasm, competition, passion, energy, courage, protection, victory, anything requiring assertiveness, standing up for yourself, or a 'fighting spirit', determination, vitality, sexuality, self-confidence, men's power, men's mysteries, drive, ambition, achievement, triumph, masculinity.

WEDNESDAY ★ Mercury
Gemini & Virgo

Education, travel, exams, study, communication, making connections, thinking, dealing with siblings, writing and speaking, knowledge, learning, adaptability, charm, youth, absorbing information.

THURSDAY ★ Jupiter
Sagittarius & Pisces

Increase and expansion of anything (remember to be careful what you wish for), luck, growth, influence, worldly power, accomplishment, fulfilment, gambling, philosophy, higher education, abundance, optimism.

FRIDAY ★ Venus
Taurus & Libra

Love, luxury, the arts, indulgence, beauty, marriage, money, prosperity, fertility, women's power, women's mysteries, grace, charm, appeal, hope, pleasure, decorating, self-worth, self-esteem, personal values, business partnerships, romance, creativity, sharing, bonding.

SATURDAY ★ Saturn
Capricorn & Aquarius

Long-term goals, career, institutions, establishments, security, investments, karma, reversal, structure, protection, solitude, privacy, determination, ending, blocking, renewing, transforming, anything to do with the public.

SUNDAY ★ Sun
Leo

All-purpose, success, wishes, generosity, happiness, optimism, spirit/essence, recognition, health, vitality, material wealth, invoking a god's aid or guidance, personal empowerment, spirituality, the Divine masculine.

YOUR NATAL MOON PHASE

Although this book is aimed at enhancing your life through the energy of your Sun sign, a bit of Lunar help can give your wishing a boost! As well as using the planetary days and hours system to add a bit of zest to your wish fulfilment, try combining your Sun sign's power periods with your natal Moon phase (your natal Moon phase can be calculated using a number of sources on the internet, or through an astrologer), or even studying which constellation the Moon is situated in at certain times, to increase the power of your spells and asking rituals. For example, you might like to 'ask' for a promotion at work during a New/Waxing Moon period, particularly if the Moon happens to fall under an auspicious sign for career advancement, such as Capricorn. Your natal Moon phase can also be used to similar effect, by researching when your Moon phase will coincide with a certain Lunar constellation position.

In most astrological interpretations the Sun is regarded as the most important, central feature of a natal chart. But to many the Moon is equally, if not more, important than the Sun sign. Many ancient cultures considered the Moon sign to be more significant. The Moon passes through the 12 signs about every 2.5 days, usually covering the whole zodiac in around 27.3 days. The Moon symbolises our inner world, the world of feeling, emotions, habitual responses, instincts, intuition, security and the subconscious. It describes our nurturing style and needs, our emotional response to life, our attitudes and likely reactions to others, our instinctive and habitual responses, the receptive feminine side of ourselves, our experience of our mother or mother figure, and our childhood experience. It represents the soul. In relationships it symbolises how we like to be nurtured and cared for, and the potential depth of our involvement on personal intimate levels.

For many centuries, people across the world have recognised that the Moon influences the affairs of all living things on planet Earth. The waxing Moon appears to have a drawing, increasing and enhancing effect, whereas the waning Moon has a decreasing, receding and withdrawing effect. All things that come into being are stamped with the qualities of the prevailing Moon stage. It seems that people born during certain Lunar phases tend to share specific attributes with other people born during this same phase. In turn, their attributes will be subtly different from those of individuals born during any of the other stages in the Moon cycle. Knowing exactly which phase of the Moon you were born under gives you all kinds of extraordinarily valuable insights into your character, emotions, behaviour and motivations in life. It can make you aware of your deepest underlying drives, the fundamental purpose that you are drawn towards in life and the contribution you can make to others and society during the course of your lifetime. This knowledge may enable you to intuit and make the most of your own personal cyclical pattern that you go through each month, and allow you to know when the most auspicious periods of time are for you and your affairs, nurture yourself and channel your energies in the most positive directions.

Because this Lunar pattern repeats itself every month, you will find that you can even pace yourself on a long-term basis. This will enable you to effectively target your efforts and goals on periods of time that you know will be potentially fortunate for you. You may in fact find that your birth phase corresponds with the days of the month when you have abundant energy, feel inspired and can generate new ideas with ease. During this period, you should work towards the fruition of your efforts, bring your dreams into light and reach for the stars!

The Lunar Phases Are:

★ New Moon
★ First/Waxing Crescent
★ First Quarter
★ Waxing Gibbous Moon
★ Full Moon
★ Waning Gibbous / Disseminating Moon
★ Last Quarter
★ Waning Crescent / Balsamic Moon
★ Back to the New Moon

SPELLS, MAGIC & WISHING WITH MOON PHASES

Though the Moon has eight astronomical phases, it is the three phases corresponding to maiden, mother and crone that are the most significant in spells, ritual, wish magic and psychic work. By tuning into the physical Moon we can understand and harness these distinct energy phases in our daily lives and magical worlds. The four primary Lunar phases are the New Moon, First Quarter, Full Moon and the Last Quarter. Depending on what sort of spell you wish to perform, your spell should take place during one of these cycles or time periods. Each phase of the Moon is good for some types of magic, but not so much for others.

NEW MOON, WAXING & FIRST QUARTER

In astronomical terms, the New Moon occurs when the Moon rises and sets at the same time as the Sun. Both bodies are found in the same position compared with the Earth. Therefore, a Solar eclipse can only ever occur at the New Moon, when the two luminaries are found, for a short time, in a perfect line relative to the Earth, with the Moon positioned between the Sun and the Earth. The New Moon's sunlit face is hidden from the Earth.

In astrological terms, the New Moon occurs at a time when the Sun and the Moon are found in the same degree of the zodiac and therefore occupy the same zodiac sign, forming a conjunction, or a 'fusing' of energies.

In astronomical terms, the First Quarter occurs seven days after the New Moon. Seen from the Earth, this phase makes the Moon like a crescent, forming the shape of a capital D.

In astrological terms, it occurs when the Sun and the Moon form a ninety-degree angle, or the square aspect, inside the zodiac, the Moon always preceding the Sun.

As the New Moon marks the beginning of a new cycle, it symbolises fresh starts. This is an exceptional time to work magic and make wishes for new beginnings, and for the conception and initiation of new projects. Use this Moon phase for improving health, the gradual increase of prosperity, attracting good luck, fertility magic, finding new love, friendship or romance, job hunting, making plans for the future and increasing your general spiritual or psychic awareness.

Overall, the Waxing Crescent and First Quarter Moon phases are appropriate for spells, rituals and workings that involve growth, healing and increase. This is a period of time lasting approximately two weeks, to draw things toward you and increase things, such as love, prosperity and new opportunities. During this period is the time to bless new projects, anything that requires energy to grow, such as gardens, business ventures, new homes, or educational pursuits. Personal growth and healing are accented, as is 'attraction magic' - drawing something to you such as love, abundance, health, success or a new path - and if done well, you can expect results by the next Full Moon. Magical workings for gain, increase or bringing things to you should be initiated when the Moon is waxing (or New, going from Dark to Full). A time for divination of all kinds, spells of spiritual intention, and for any creative project you wish to see birthed, with magical and fruitful results.

While making a wish within the first forty-eight hours after the New Moon is a powerful way of helping it come to fruition, the most potent time for making wishes is actually within the first eight hours of the exact time of its position. Write down your wish list within this first eight hours on a piece of appropriately coloured paper with a special writing tool, and be sure to capture the essence of your wish by wording it in a way that charges your emotions and simply feels 'right'. Make a maximum of ten wishes (less is perfectly fine too), as making too many wishes might disperse their energy too much to be effective. After writing down your list and releasing your wishes to the Universe in whichever form you feel happy with, keep your list and check on it in a few days', weeks' or months' time to assess whether anything has shifted in the direction of your listed dreams, desires or goals. I'll bet it has - or at the very least, something even better has arrived in its place!

Although the first forty-eight hours after the New Moon is the most potent time to make a special wish, you can begin Waxing Moon magic when you can see the crescent in the sky and continue until the day before the Full Moon. The closer to the Full Moon, the more intense the energies. In fact, a personally devised ritual using any special Lunar-associated materials over three days up to and including the Full Moon is excellent for something you require urgently or within a short timeframe.

In some cultures, people turn over silver coins or jewellery three times when the crescent Moon appears in the sky and make a wish. As the Moon grows, it is believed that prosperity and good fortune will grow too.

While the New Moon is not known as a time for 'banishing' or releasing things we no longer want in our lives, I feel that if we are to ask and wish for things, we need to make room to receive them. Making room means that the Universe can slot it right into our lives where we have cleared our paths for it. Clutter, unwanted things, unhappy relationships, possessions that no longer serve us, are all things we can banish. So, to help what you are asking for come into your life quicker, the New Moon is a particularly opportune time to throw a few things out so you can make way for the new and clear up some space for that which you are wishing for. What are you waiting for? Start creating a space for your wishes today!

FULL MOON

In astronomical terms, the Full Moon occurs 14 days after the New Moon, on the day when the Moon sets at the same time the Sun rises, or conversely. The two luminaries are effectively facing each other, with the Earth in between, the Sun shining its light onto the reflective Moon, giving it the fully lit up appearance of a giant, bright, perfectly round sphere. Indeed, its entire face is bathed in sunlight. A Lunar eclipse can only occur at the Full Moon, when the Sun, Moon and Earth are all in line, and the Earth hides the lit side of the Moon to us.

In astrological terms, a Full Moon occurs at the time when the Sun and Moon are 180 degrees apart inside the zodiac, and therefore positioned in opposite signs, forming an opposition aspect.

The highest energy occurs at the Full Moon, making this is a powerful time for all manner of magical workings. Use the Full Moon phase for any immediate need, a sudden boost of power or courage, psychic protection, a change of career or location, travel, healing acute health conditions, the consummation of love or a commitment, justice, ambition and promotion of all kinds. This phase lasts approximately 3 days - 24 hours before the exact Full Moon, the day of, and 24 hours after it, according to many sources - giving us 3 full days to perform our spells. However, we are not strictly limited to a three-day period; the power of this phase can actually be accessed for seven days - three days prior to, the night of, and the three days after the Full Moon. The Full Moon period is when the Moon is at her most powerful, being the most luminous and radiant part of the cycle. Known as the 'high tide' of psychic power, the Full Moon represents culmination, climax, fulfilment and abundance. The Full Moon governs all kinds of magic, including manifestation, banishing, and is particularly good for calling forth protection and heightening your intuitive abilities. The Full Moon contains magic that calls forth personal power, fertility, spiritual development, and psychic awareness. Cleansing of ritual tools, crystals, wish lists, Tarot decks, and the like can be done during this phase. Magic worked during the Full Moon often takes one complete cycle to come to fruition. Try also reaffirming your desires during the New Moon to give them an added nudge in the right direction.

LAST QUARTER OR WANING MOON

In astronomical terms, the Last Quarter, or Waning Moon, occurs twenty-one days after the New Moon. The time difference between the rising and setting of the two luminaries is reduced to what it was at the First Quarter. Viewed from the Earth, the Moon resembles a crescent whose lit up area is decreasing in size, forming the shape of a capital C.

In astrological terms, the Waning Moon occurs when the Sun and Moon are positioned at ninety degree angles of each other in the zodiac, forming the square aspect again. However, during this phase, the Sun is instead *ahead* of the Moon.

The Waning Moon represents the Lunar cycle from Full to Dark. Any spells and magic performed during this period is based purely around banishing and releasing. It could involve releasing things which no longer serve you (such as behaviours, material things, relationships and attitudes), banishing negative energies, and removing obstacles which are standing in the way of achieving your goals or dreams. The Waning Moon is the best time for cleansing, gently releasing, eliminating, expelling and completion. It is of great assistance when you are wanting to let go of something, or someone, gradually. The Dark of the Moon, the period when the Moon is no longer visible to the naked eye, until the New Moon, is the most useful time for divination of all kinds.

★ What is your natal Moon phase type? Can you think of ways you can combine it with the power of your Sun sign to effect change and bring about wonderful happenings? ★

HARNESSING YOUR PERSONAL MOON MAGIC ★ MOON IN LEO

When the Moon is in your sign of Leo, it is a great time for working magic around: Self-confidence, radiance, personal power, leadership, generosity, benevolence, strength, courage and success of all kinds. Suggested operations could be around rituals and spells to increase your authority and command of others, gold, positive thinking, optimism, winning, success, and learning to be an effective, loyal and kind-hearted leader. With the Moon in Leo, you can also seek to create drama out of acting or other theatrical pursuits, spend time with children, and increase time spent enjoying fun, leisure, pleasure, and good food and company. This Moon accentuates one's ability to shine, so try and capitalise on any talents you have during this period.

THE MOON ★ WHAT IT REPRESENTS IN THE HUMAN PSYCHE & NATAL CHART

The Moon in the sky shines with the reflected light of the Sun. Although not a planet, the Moon is our nearest celestial neighbour and exerts a great influence upon us. The gravitational pull of the Moon affects our body fluids, which contribute to about 90 per cent of our biological make-up. It moves at approximately half a degree per hour and takes an average of 27.3 days to pass through all twelve zodiac signs, staying in each for around 2.5 days.

In astrology the Moon corresponds with the way in which we reflect and respond to what is going on around us. It has to do with our feelings, emotions and instincts and, in the same way the Moon influences the tides on planet Earth, it symbolises the ebb and flow of our emotional nature, our moods, fluctuations and changeability. The Moon is the archetype of the Mother, which is within us all, and represents the primary feminine principle in the natal chart. It is through the Moon that we express our parental instincts - caring, nurturing, protecting, sensitivity. The Moon has links with the past and the subconscious and it is from this almost primitive source that our natural instinctual forces flow.

The Moon is essentially a feminine principle and associates with the inner personality, receptivity, passivity and inward-oriented feelings. It can act as an inner guide to the deeper self, the unconscious self, figures half-shrouded in mystery, linking the hidden personal world of the subconscious to the clearer world of personal awareness.

The Moon is the innermost core of our being, private feelings, habitual reactions and subconscious habits. It is the caring, nurturing sustainer of life, the 'mother' of the zodiac. It tells us about how we seek security, our urge to nurture, our nurturing style, our responses and feelings and moods. The innermost core of our being, private feelings, subconscious habits. It is concerned with habits, mothering, habitual/instinctive responses and personality. It is our karma, our soul, our past.

The Moon represents our mother or mother figure, our feminine side, maternal instinct, our nurturing style and needs, our unconscious self, our emotional reactions, the subconscious, our feelings, instincts, intuition, receptivity, habits, what we need to feel secure, fluctuations, cycles, moods, and our childhood. Its position in the birth chart is very significant, because as well as revealing feminine qualities and the potential gentleness and tenderness of a being, the Moon also reveals important information about the experiences and expression of the five senses

The Moon is essentially receptive and passive; it reflects the life experience rather than initiating it. Fluctuating and cyclical, the Moon is the planet (although technically a satellite) of the childhood experience, and instinctual reactions. It represents the mother (a child's experience and expectations of their mother), maternal instincts and the feminine principle, indicating how strongly these manifest in an individual, male or female.

As it represents what our childhood experience is likely to be, and childhood is essentially a time where our consciousness has not yet fully developed, our Moon sign traits seem to be more apparent in our younger years. We will usually show our Moon sign traits more so than our Sun sign traits during this developing period of infancy and early childhood, until we have the presence of mind to more consciously develop our ego and true core self (the Sun).

The symbol for the Moon ☽ is a representation of its crescent in its waxing phase from new to full, but it can also be seen as two half circles - these form a bowl shape, a receptacle, a feminine container that 'receives' and 'holds' anything put into it. The half circle, unlike the full circle of the Sun, is finite and incomplete, almost as if striving for wholeness.

The Moon represents our *soul*.

YOUR MOON SIGN

The Sun / Moon Polarity
Conscious & Unconscious, Night & Day, Yin & Yang

Man does, woman is.
Edward Edinger

Your Moon Sign, representing your soul, and your Sun sign, representing your spirit, work together to form the foundation of your basic personality, expression and nature. If you know what your Moon sign is, look it up below and read how it works with your Leo Sun to blend your mind, soul and spirit.

♈ **With the Moon in ARIES, Sun in Leo**, you are likely to be ★ Confident, brave, passionate, adventurous, elf-interested, vain, active, rash, honourable, dramatic, proud, boastful, overbearing, pompous, enthusiastic, generous, domineering, affectionate, all-embracing, impressive, extroverted, independent, egocentric, approval-seeking, honest, inspirational, whole-hearted, loyal, adventurous, hot-tempered, dazzling, a show-off, charismatic, a leader, courageous, assertive, temperamental, insensitive, playful, ambitious, theatrical, self-reliant, energetic, emotionally bold and reckless, restless, speak before thinking, pioneering, original, forward-looking, lively, fun, bright, an individualist, one who has moral integrity, flamboyant, and prone to grandiosity.

Sun/Moon Harmony Rating ★ *8 out of 10* **

♉ **With the Moon in TAURUS, Sun in Leo,** you are likely to be ★ Level-headed, pragmatic, dictatorial, productive, bossy, strong, brave, a leader, proud, determined, possessive, stubborn, generous, materialistic, patient, regal, luxury-loving, subjective, steady-paced, opinionated, tenacious, devoted, stoic, faithful, magnetic, seeking of power, artistic, self-seeking, loyal, friendly, robust, capable, resourceful, extravagant, dependable, demanding, unflappable, entrepreneurial, ambitious, peace-loving but strong-willed, philanthropic, realistic, sensible, persistent, commanding, dedicated and loving of grandeur.

Sun/Moon Harmony Rating ★ *6.5 out of 10*

♊ **With the Moon in GEMINI, Sun in Leo,** you are likely to be ★ Changeable, friendly, bright, lively, zestful, effervescent, sociable, versatile, quick-witted, flippant, charismatic, an opportunist, perceptive, clever, a perennial student of life, approachable, charming, inspiring, honourable but light-hearted, playful, stimulating, warm-hearted, optimistic, resilient, occasionally unruly and fickle, flexible yet stubborn, iconoclastic, popular, curious, emotionally impulsive, restless, inconsistently creative, a people person, warmly spontaneous, aspiring, youthfully spirited, communicative, socially aware, childish, gifted, intellectual, theatrical, a wonderful friend, funny, fun, impressionable, flirtatious, adaptable, open to new ideas, adventurous, bold, reluctant to face the darker aspects of life, too busy to deal with feelings, and ruled equally by your head and your heart.

Sun/Moon Harmony Rating ★ *8.5 out of 10*

♋ **With the Moon in CANCER, Sun in Leo,** you are likely to be ★ Proud of family, sensitive, intuitive, emotionally expressive, jealous, ardent, dramatic, loving of home and family, temperamental, torn between introversion and extroversion, affectionate, understanding, vulnerable, in possession of a vast inner strength, aesthetically sensitive, ardent, passionately tender, distorted, anxious, self-absorbed, tenacious, devoted, compassionate, sulky, clingy, reflective, possessive, kind-hearted, dedicated, imaginative, creative, gentle-spirited, optimistic, hopeful, faithful, colourful, moody, clannish, dependable, receptive, loyal, conflicted between personal privacy and outer involvement with others, a sensitive individualist, protective of self and others, and occasionally moved to emotional tantrums.

Sun/Moon Harmony Rating ★ *6.5 out of 10*

♌ **With the Moon in LEO, Sun in Leo,** you are likely to be ★ Generous, proud, vain, pompous, extraverted, individualistic, strong, courageous, visionary, brave, fearless, bold, artistic, playful, affectionate, arrogant, generous, passionate, impetuous, radiant enthusiastic, a good leader, romantic, inspirational, charismatic, commanding, warm, demanding, open, regal, powerful, charming, extroverted, honest, single-minded, magnanimous, inclined to get carried away by romance and drama, direct, expressive, ambitious, creative, artistic, flamboyant, prone to sulking, uplifting, attention-seeking, dignified, emotionally radiating warmth, idealistic, luxury-loving, extravagant, demonstrative, inflexible, gullible and authoritative.

Sun/Moon Harmony Rating ★ *8 out of 10*

♍ **With the Moon in VIRGO, Sun in Leo,** you are likely to be ★ Intelligent, judgemental, cool, calm and collected, charming, down-to-Earth yet dramatic, purposeful, discerning, discriminating, a commanding perfectionist, methodical, studious, highly moral, prudish, high-minded, helpful, a striver for excellence, pushy, defiant, articulate, aspiring, dogged, thorough, self-critical, fussy, serious but warm, kind-hearted, dutiful, self-contained, considerate, respectful, mentally alert, efficient, a good organiser, mentally dextrous, pedantic, genuine, choosy, caring, stubborn, wild-at-heart yet conventional, obsessive compulsive, spirited yet grounded, objectively rational, cool-headed, conflicted between being the king or the king's servant, willing to help and do what needs to be done, altruistic, bright, devoted, dry-witted, in possession of high standards, and feisty yet uptight.

Sun/Moon Harmony Rating ★ *5.5 out of 10*

♎ **With the Moon in LIBRA, Sun in Leo,** you are likely to be ★ Sociable, people-loving, glamorous, artistic, aesthetically aware, luxury-seeking, attractive, refined, easy going, affectionate, loving, charismatic, indecisive, charming, popular, graceful, pleasure-seeking, regally friendly, eager to engage, reasonable, smooth, fair, diplomatic, stylish, idealistic, vain, unconsciously snobbish, prone to laziness, procrastinating, approachable, tolerant, distanced from your true emotional power, civilised, sharing, gracious, cooperative, approval-seeking, outgoing, hospitable, hedonistic, indecisive, interested in people, romantically idealistic, endearing, delightful, colourfully persuasive, artistically sensitive, emotionally naïve, and conflicted between self-reliance and needing others.

Sun/Moon Harmony Rating ★ *9 out of 10*

♏ **With the Moon in SCORPIO, Sun in Leo,** you are likely to be ★ Dramatic, defiant, powerfully instinctive, theatrical, intense, powerful, forceful, commanding, magnetic, complex, dangerous, feisty, highly charged, extreme, possessive, keenly insightful, loyal, investigative, charismatic, imperious, unbending, fanatical, shrewd, strong-willed, dominating, intensely dedicated, passionate, unyielding, resourceful, resilient, controlling, ambitious, proud, insatiable, sceptical, a survivor, stubborn, influential, persevering, thorough, devoted, courageous, emotionally expressive, an astute observer, perceptive, self-reliant, dogmatic, exacting, potentially ruthless and dictatorial, manipulative, and emotionally powerful.

Sun/Moon Harmony Rating ★ *7.5 out of 10*

♐ **With the Moon in SAGITTARIUS, Sun in Leo,** you are likely to be ★ Eager, adventurous, impractical, gregarious, independent, idealistic, zestful, inspiring, big-hearted, honest, insensitive, impatient, prone to preach, arrogant, unaware of the subtleties of social intercourse, outspoken, generous, sincere, a visionary, boastful, philosophical, able to see the 'big picture', emotionally reckless, pompous, bold, a free spirit, non-committal, a good leader, confident, enthusiastic, positive, sarcastic, direct, in possession of a crazy sense of humour, far-sighted, extraverted, optimistic, a lover of learning, outrageous, aspiring, gregarious, ambitious, sociable, warm, thoughtless, broad-minded, expansive, verbose, theatrical, dramatic, freedom-seeking, and guided by reason rather than emotion.

Sun/Moon Harmony Rating ★ *8.5 out of 10* **

♑ **With the Moon in CAPRICORN, Sun in Leo,** you are likely to be ★ Dependable, practical, steadfast, resourceful, committed, independent, driven to succeed, ambitious, purposeful, stubborn, wilful, persevering, guarded, self-protective, critical, cool-headed, wise, determined, harsh, direct, diligent, shrewd, organised, down-to-Earth, an excellent leader, efficient, authoritative, serious, highly moral, courageous, impatient with imperfection, sensible, materialistic, understanding of practical applications and wisdom, tense, self-controlled, personally honourable, highly principled, fearless, uptight, socially rigid, self-contained, sardonically humorous, a workaholic, a practical visionary, self-demanding, sprightly yet sombre, and domineering.

Sun/Moon Harmony Rating ★ *6 out of 10*

♒ **With the Moon in AQUARIUS, Sun in Leo,** you are likely to be ★ Warm yet cool, friendly, tolerant, frank, independent, freedom-seeking, idealistic, emotionally detached yet romantic, eccentrically theatrical, vain yet vulnerable, unconventional, paradoxical, imaginative, opinionated, honest, loyal, original, forward-moving, inventive, impersonal in relationships, highly observant, strongly social, loving of friendship and groups, individualistic, in possession of deep convictions, flamboyant or bohemian, an objective and visionary leader, optimistic, vividly imaginative, aristocratic, truthful, proud, endearing, idiosyncratic, perceptive, broad-minded, acutely aware of the human condition, progressive, scientifically oriented, objective, living an unusual lifestyle in some way, well-intentioned, open to the unusual, emotionally naïve, over-identifying with causes, blunt and insensitive when comparing people with your ideals, unorthodox, impractical, humanitarian, globally aware, courageous and committed to your ideals, and in possession of an eternal sense of hope and belief in human potential.

Sun/Moon Harmony Rating ★ *7.5 out of 10*

♓ **With the Moon in PISCES, Sun in Leo,** you are likely to be ★ Intuitive, generous, highly imaginative, gregarious, able to blend objectivity with mysticism, devoted, self-indulgent, escapist, aware of beauty and tragedy, prone to dejection, emotionally unsettled, caring, open, overly idealistic, a chaser of spiritual rainbows, hearty, good-natured, intriguing, kind, modest yet proud, charismatic, endearing, charming, able to be introverted or extraverted as called for, emotionally expressive, warmly sentimental, understanding, self-assured yet vulnerable, a dramatist, a poet, altruistic, humorous, receptive, artistic, creative, pleasure-seeking, mysterious, empathetic, people-pleasing, impressionable, easily swayed, gullible, impractical, evasive, perceptive, emotionally charged, and aware of the needs of others.

Sun/Moon Harmony Rating ★ *8 out of 10*

** If your Moon is in Aries or Sagittarius, your Sun and Moon will form what is known in astrology as a trine aspect. This aspect is the easiest, most flowing and harmonious astrological aspect, ensuring that your Sun and Moon, or spirit and soul, are well integrated. With both luminaries in Fire signs, this gives them the best possible degree of complementary energy - a blending of the elements suggests a balanced expression of personality. One drawback of the trine aspect lies in the fact that its easy flow can be *too* harmonious; if our path is too smooth and difficulties don't arise to challenge us from time to time, we can often become lazy and complacent, stunting our growth and spiritual evolution. As Fire signs, you share the art of vitality, zest, enthusiasm, broad-mindedness, affability, idealism, independence, drive, ambition, force, affection, warm-heartedness, generosity, sociability, and have extravagant tastes, but may be temperamental, dramatic, overbearing, egocentric, restless, bossy, insensitive, careless, arrogant and self-centred

YOUR BODY & HEALTH

"A physician without a knowledge of astrology has
no right to call himself a physician."
Hippocrates (born c. 460 BC)

Hippocrates, the fifth century BC Greek physician and 'father of medicine' and supposed author of the Hippocratic Oath, maintained that no one should be allowed to practise medicine who had not first studied astrology. Another Greek physician, Claudius Galen, brought together a huge range of knowledge and ideas in the second century AD which dominated medical practice until the 17th century. Among his teachings was a diagnostic technique which assumed that illnesses and their treatments were affected by and governed by the phases of the Moon. For centuries, astrology was a compulsory component of medical training (and still is in some natural medicine degrees), albeit only one aspect of diagnosis and treatment.

Medical or health astrology concerns particular ways of determining and interpreting an individual's horoscope with particular reference to health issues - diagnosis of current dis-eases, identification of areas of bodily weaknesses, and the prescription of natural cures and remedies. In ancient times, and still even today, the movement of the stars and planets was believed to affect bodily functions, and to cause ailments, or cure them.

During the Middle Ages, many drawings of the 'zodiac man' were made, which showed which signs of the zodiac were related to each part of the body, providing information as to the best times of the year to undertake cures for ailments affecting the corresponding body parts.

Health astrology persists today in many forms and among astrologers themselves, from whom clients seek counsel on health-related issues, and while it certainly cannot be used diagnose a condition or dis-ease, one's Sun sign, along with other factors of the natal chart, can definitely indicate potential problem areas of weakness or possible troubles. This branch of astrology has been found to be surprisingly accurate in most cases. While mostly accurate, none of the following information should ever be used as a substitute for professional medical advice should you be personally concerned about any of the conditions or afflictions listed for your Sun sign.

LEONINE HEALTH

Leo is associated with the Heart, Back, Spine, Upper Back, Forearms, Dorsal Vertebrae, Aorta and Wrists. The Superior and Inferior Vena Cava, and the Blood is also a domain of Leo's, and the blood, coupled with the heart, are the providers and the sustainers of life.

The vitality of Leo is usually boundless, and they have the ability to absorb the vivifying power of the Sun to the fullest extent; sunshine, coupled with fresh air, is their finest tonic and restorative. Being a Fire sign, Leos are prone to high fevers, sudden illnesses and accidents. You are also, perhaps due to your extravagant, indulgent and active lifestyle, prone to heart conditions, cardiovascular issues, back injury and pain, and even spinal injuries. You should not overindulge in strenuous physical activity either, as this can put a strain on the heart. The heart, spine, back and eyes are the parts of the body most liable to afflictions or injury. Curvature of the spine, angina, irregular heartbeat, palpitations, hypertension, heart dis-ease, and back problems in general often afflict Leo. Circulatory problems, meningitis and eye diseases are Leo's other common complaints. Generally speaking, the heart is usually exceptionally strong and healthy in Leo people and you are usually capable of enormous exertion (if in sound health) without any ill effects.

The typical Leo is never down for long, seeing incapacitation as a sign of weakness. And although you are normally vital, you can burn yourself out every now and again through exhaustion. Naturally energetic, you should also guard against being idle or under-occupied as you can become morose and gloomy, which further affects your health and energy levels. In fact, your health difficulties may well centre around those parts of the body that control the vitality of it. Leo affects the concentration of energy. Your nature is hot, dry and excessive. Principal rulerships are, as already mentioned, the heart (both physically and energetically), the spinal column's nerves and marrow, the spine (especially T3 and T4, over the heart), blood (as a carrier of energy), spleen, and the circulatory system (over which your opposite sign Aquarius rules).

Possessing the most robust constitution of the zodiac, you are theoretically and arguably the healthiest of all the signs. Your nerves, muscles and vital organs are usually arranged in a fine functional balance, and your fiery, outgoing temperament gives you the will to survive - and *thrive* - in the most challenging situations.

You throw off illnesses very rapidly, such are your extraordinary powers of recuperation. Fortunately, the Leo temperament is largely sanguine and positive, so you are usually able to snap out of depression or despondency relatively quickly.

You seldom suffer from chronic or lingering conditions, although periodic eye trouble can be a complaint. When illness strikes, it is usually sudden and swift. As a patient, you are inclined to require a lot of attention and, being naturally melodramatic, frequently convince yourself you are in worse shape than you are. At first, you may find it wonderful to be given the opportunity to rest, but this rapidly turns into boredom and restlessness.

A distinct danger period for Leo-born people occurs in middle age. At this stage of life, the superb nervous system that served you so well in your youth is easily upset. At this time more than ever, it is important to relax and not to react automatically to every emotional situation. In the space of even an hour, your moods and whims can fluctuate, and you are likely to get heated up over the most trivial provocations.

Diet-wise, you have a natural liking of rich and extravagant foods, and the heart being one of your most vulnerable areas, you should watch what you eat and ensure it is heart-enriching and sustaining. Indeed, your great fondness for pleasure can be a health hazard in itself, as you are also an inveterate party-goer, exposing yourself to the dangers of drinking or eating to excess.

To use an analogy, although you have a loud roar and fearsome image, you are really just a kitten at heart. You are psychologically fearless in the face of danger and well-equipped to cope with physical pain. Underneath the bravado, you are a sensitive soul who can fight to the death in defence if necessary, but you may protest at a pinprick and perhaps even faint while having your blood taken.

Your ruling body, the Sun, affects the Brain, Heart, Spleen, Sinews, Circulatory System, Cells, the Back, Spinal Cord and the right-hand side of the body, and you may experience issues, conditions, afflictions or injuries in any or all of these parts of the body. It also governs the thymus and endocrine gland, and is connected with the body's immune system. The Sun shows vitality, the 'life force', and natural strength of constitution. Solar-ruled weak spots, where dis-ease is most like to occur, are related to the circulation, the blood, the spine, the heart and the eyes.

Keeping yourself in excellent health overall, with a special awareness of Leo's vulnerable points, is key to achieving all you set out to do, and getting the most out of your life!

★ The Spiritual Heart ★

"The heart is a common organ, and rather humble, too. It works unceasingly throughout our lives, never speaking in words or equations, yet carrying the spark of the Divine within. The brain thinks, but the heart knows. The brain analyses, disassembles and reassembles the patterns found in the past, while the heart feels into the future. The heart trusts, carrying us forward into what can be. This is the essence (of the heart), carrying the spiritual pattern of human destiny, our highest future."

Robert Simmons, *Stones of the New Consciousness*

THE CELL SALTS ★ ASTROLOGICAL TONICS

Homeopathy and astrology have colluded to provide a wonderful list of astrological tonics, one particularly suited to each of the twelve signs. These are called 'homeopathic cell salts', 'tissue salts' or 'biochemic cell salts', and are available in most health food stores, are inexpensive and easy to take. They are considered to be gentle, effective and safe, even for children, people in fragile health states, and the elderly. Although the full picture, drawn from a full natal horoscope, gives a fuller, more accurate idea of an individual's unique constitution, even simply working with one's date of birth can be enough for the medical astrologer to suggest the use of a cell salt based upon the correlation with an individual's Sun sign.

As well as the cell salts having a significant effect upon physical ailments, they can also profoundly influence the subtle energy bodies, including the mental, emotional, etheric and spiritual. Although the most common use of these salts is based upon each salt's correspondence with a Sun sign, use of the cell salt related to one's Moon sign can assist with addressing deeper underlying emotional issues, such as anxiety, depression, panic and fear. Use of the cell salt relating to your Moon sign will therefore help to restore your sense of safety, balance, security and emotional resilience. In the first seven years of life, when the Moon is the most influential sphere in our lives, Lunar cell salts are the most appropriate choice as a remedy or tonic.

For specific health problems, take both the salt of your Sun or Moon sign, *and* the salt that pertains to the specific condition. The same principle applies to the Ascendant sign, as the First House represents one's physical health, and especially if the Sun or Moon is a rising planet, which means rulership of the whole chart. For the purposes of this book, however, the cell salt that correlates with your Sun sign only is outlined.

TISSUE SALT FOR LEO ★ MAG PHOS.

Magnesium Phosphoricum, or Mag Phos. (Magnesium phosphate) is the cell salt for Leo. Leos need this cell salt to restore their nervous force and muscular vigour. Along with Kali Phos., this tissue salt is a principle nerve tonic and remedy. Painful menstrual cramps can be effectively eased by using this salt. An infrastructure constituent, physiologically Mag Phos. can help prevent heart attacks and epileptic crises. Mag Phos. has a longstanding tradition of use in conditions involving cramps, nerves, convulsions or spasms. It can be used as a pain-reliever and is even regarded as a natural aspirin without the side effects. As Leo rules the heart, cardiac system, spine, diaphragm and upper back, Mag Phos. can help alleviate any conditions afflicting these areas, such as cramps, tics, spasms, aches and pains, muscular twitching, hiccoughs, convulsions and even paralysis. As Mag Phos. can be found in beer and cereals, it might be interesting to note that a craving for beer can mean a deficiency in this mineral. Foods high in this mineral salt are citrus, oats, cabbage, lettuce, peas, apples, plums, wheat bran, beetroot and cocoa.

FIRE SIGN LEO & THE CHOLERIC HUMOR

Greek physician Hippocrates (460 - 370 BC) theorised that certain human behaviours were caused by body fluids, called 'humours'. Later, Galen of Pergamon (AD 131 - 200), a Greek physician, developed the first typology of temperaments to encompass many facets of the human psyche and physiology. These also related to the classical elements of Fire, Earth, Air and Water - as choleric, melancholic, sanguine and phlegmatic respectively. According to the Greeks who developed the temperament theory (the word stems from the Latin word *temperamentum*, meaning mixture), temperament is the 'mixture' of qualities that combine to form elements in physics and humours in medicine. The Greeks sought equilibrium in the four qualities of hot, cold, wet (moist), and dry, the elements of Earth, Air, Fire and Water, and the four humours of choler or yellow bile, melancholier or black bile, blood and phlegm. If balance was achieved, the person was said to be well- or even-tempered, and the importance of determining the temperament allowed for imbalances to be treated.

In ancient times, each of the four types of humours corresponded to a different personality type, which were associated with a domination of various biological functions. It was suggested that the temperaments came to clearest manifestation in childhood, between around the ages of six and fourteen of age, after which they become subordinate, but still influential, factors in our personality. It is important to note that your temperament is not your personality. However, your personality can incorporate parts of the temperament in its expression. Personality is shaped by both external and internal factors, whereas the temperament is innate, an inborn, inherent part of each individual.

The Fire element corresponds with the humour choleric, which is characterised by a short response time-delay, but response sustained for a relatively long time. Driven by their goals, for which they will use others as tools to achieve them, a choleric disposition represents touchiness, restlessness, aggression, spirit, excitement, changeability, impulsiveness, activity and optimism.

Choleric is associated with the ego level of self. Its taste is salty and sour, its nature acidic, its indication yellow bile. The choleric humour is associated with the astral body ^ *, and with hot and dry conditions.

Additionally, the ethereal (or vital) body, comprises four ethers or subtle fluids, which are governed by the four Fixed signs of the zodiac: Taurus, Leo, Scorpio and Aquarius. Leo corresponds to the *light ether*, which controls blood circulation, cardiac rhythm and the functioning of the five senses.

^ A couple of thousand years ago, the Mesopotamians, Chinese and Egyptians, and more recently the Arabs, practised a medicine called 'of three bodies'. According to the doctors of the ancient world (who often practised as astrologers as well), a human being had three bodies: the physical body, the ethereal (or vital) body and the astral body, imparting a holistic approach to health. In modern medicine, usually only the physical body is focused upon fully. According to tradition, this physical body comprises three principles or states corresponding to three primordial elements: *solid* (Earth), *liquid* (Water) and *gas* (Air). This is the material body, the physical outer cover of muscles, nerves and organs held together by the skeleton. The Fire element corresponds with the *astral* body, which sits outside the physical body in one's auric field.

* The primordial element linked to the astral body is Fire, and it includes seven points, or doors, of perception which correspond exactly with the chakras. The astral body has a degree of vibration and radiance which is far higher than that of the ethereal body, an area which sits just beyond the physical body in one's auric field. Ancient physicians believed that this radiance covered an area varying from 40 centimetres to three metres around the physical body, and that this area varied greatly depending on the psychic energy of the individual. (The higher the levels, the larger the area of the radiance). The astral body is described as a diffused outer layer with whirls and flashing swirls of colour which move constantly. The intensity of its colour and movement varies according to the pattern of thoughts, feelings, emotions, moods and desires of the individual.

MONEY ATTRIBUTES

Colour for Increased Earning Power ★ Gold

The following plants can be used by all zodiac signs to assist in attracting money ★ Ginger, Allspice, Clover, Orange, Marjoram, Cinnamon, Sassafras, Woodruff, Bergamot, Tonka Beans, Heliotrope, Alfalfa, Coltsfoot, Thyme, Mace, Irish Moss, Clove, Almond, Corn, Honeysuckle, Sesame, Nutmeg, Vetiver, Poppy, Jasmine, Dill and Elder Flower. To attract luck and success, try using any of the above, combined with any of the following: Alfalfa Seeds, Basil, Mustard Seeds, Vervain Leaves, Poppy Seeds, Rosemary, Lemon, Anise and Holly.

Striving for financial gain and abundance with a healthy inner moral compass is, in my view, one of the most noble goals we can set for ourselves. When we have more money, we are better placed to help ourselves and of course others; after all, as Abraham Maslow's Hierarchy of Needs model (1943) attests, once our primary and base survival needs have been satisfied, we can then advance higher towards loftier achievements, such as self-confidence, creativity and self-actualisation. Prosperity allows us to turn our attention to these more transcendental matters - to reach for lives not just of material comfort and luxuries, but of meaning, generosity, balance, harmony, fulfilment and joy. Our Sun sign can offer clues as to how we go about acquiring, earning, saving, maintaining, and allowing the overall flow of giving and receiving money. What's *your* money style?

Leos are naturally big spenders and you often live well above your means, money simply falling through your buttery gold fingers. You can be extravagant with money and occasionally indulge in excessive spending, especially if to impress others with status symbols, but this can be reined in through your Fixed, controlled nature. Your financial standing is usually good and steady, with money often coming by favour of superiors, by legacy from a 'father', or through wise investments.

You tend to spend more money than you should on decorating your 'palace' and throne. However, you have a generous heart and an innate ability to generate more than enough money for yourself and others.

If a typical Leo was asked whether fame or fortune appealed to them more, most Lions would say fame. Many Leos desire both of course, but praise and recognition for your personal and financial prowess is of vital importance to you also. Even if you do feel that fame is more important than fortune, deep down you seem to expect the fortune to follow naturally, as fame's natural complementary partner.

Your resources are usually used to benefit others, and this includes money. Although you spend lavishly when you have the money, it is not a matter of serious concern to you. If, however, it can buy you power, authority or status among your peers, you will set your sights on achieving your financial goals with gusto. You may be 'penny wise and pound foolish', so the saying goes, but you are willing to undertake almost any kind of work or enterprise to obtain the funds required to fuel your rather expensive tastes.

Money is important to you, mainly because of the things it can buy, and being extravagant and having expensive tastes, you often spend abundantly, thoughtlessly and with wild abandon. Being more concerned than most with your image, you vainly prefer designer labels and brand names over generic ones which may be more suited to your budget and future financial goals. However, you are usually willing to save up for certain things, and are lucky in that money tends to come to you freely. You are forever trying to widen your financial horizons in whatever means possible. Overall, being a luxury-seeker, you love that money can indeed buy you the lifestyle you desire - and that, to you, is the ultimate luxury.

COLOURS

Chromatomancy, or divination by colour, is a form of energy therapy that has been used for thousands of years by many different cultures. It works on the principle that we make both instinctive and rational choices or preferences based on circumstances which are already present in ourselves; colour also has an effect on the energy in an environment, and we in turn respond consciously or subconsciously to our surroundings. If we look at the causes, and try to understand the reasons, as to why we are so receptive to one particular colour over another, we will see that there is a subtle link between certain hues and our emotional and instinctive individual reactions. The colour which we give to things results from a combination of three elements:

1. The light or the vibration of a body;

2. The context in which it is found and the interaction between its own light and that of its environment;

3. The sensitivity of the eye's retina which sees the body in question. Because of this, a colour can vary, depending on the individual's perceptions, namely, his sensitivity, his mood, and his view of reality. For a long time, people have understood that their vision of reality depends a lot on their moods, feelings and emotions.

Chromatotherapy, or colour healing, stems from this body of evidence, and its main application is the use of colours for healing purposes. Colours are generally associated with characteristics, feelings, stones, metals, plants and flowers, planets and even the zodiac signs. In varying cultures, they play a significant role in ceremonies and regalia.

We vibrate to the frequency of colour, shown through its continual movement and change in our aura ^. One of the most beautiful examples of colour is the rainbow. This architect of colour is caused by the refraction and internal reflection of light in raindrops. Colour can be perceived as either a pigment, or as illumination. The colour spectrum can be divided into eight main colours: red, orange, yellow, green, turquoise, blue, violet and magenta. Each colour has a wavelength and frequency that carry different therapeutic qualities which have indirect effects upon our health and bodily systems, and because of this, coupled with the fact that we as living energy centres emanate colour, colour can be a great medium in healing, calming, energising, increasing and attracting.

Aristotle, in the fourth century BCE, considered blue and yellow to be the true primary colours and related them to life's polarities: Sun and Moon, male and female, stimulation and sedation, in and out, expansion and contraction. He also associated colours with the four elements of Fire, Earth, Air and Water. Hippocrates, the father of medicine, used colour extensively in medicinal healing and recognised that the therapeutic effects of a white violet differed from those of a purple one. In the fifteenth century, Paracelsus placed particular importance on the role of colour in healing.

Each Sun sign and planetary body has a specific colour or colours which when used in combination with wishing rituals, can enhance their power immensely. Coloured candles can be used to good effect, as the fire energy of the flame/s increases the power of any wish, and flames are also a useful aid to meditating on, focusing upon or clarifying what you want. Coloured candles help to focus the energy for whatever purpose the colour is in sympathy with (e.g. green for money, pink for romance, orange for joy, etc.)

With all this in mind, wearing or using your Sun sign or ruling planet's magical colour/s on a regular basis will undoubtedly bring great benefits.

^ The aura is defined as an energy field, which interpenetrates with, and radiates beyond, the physical body. Clairvoyantly seen, the aura is full of light, colour and shade. The trained healer or seer sees or senses indications within the aura as to the spiritual, physical and emotional state of the individual. Much of the auric colour and energy emanates from the chakras.

YOUR LUCKY COLOURS

For Leo ★ Gold, Scarlet, Orange, Deep Yellows, Royal Purple, Light Green and White

For the Sun ★ Yellow, Gold, Orange

Leo is a sign that loves glamour and strives to be bright, bold and beautiful. Appearance is therefore very important to Leos - you always dress for impact and attention. You appreciate - and look magnificent in - all bright colours!

Each of the eight colours of the rainbow spectrum also has a complementary colour to which it is matched. Red is complementary to turquoise, orange to blue, yellow to violet, and green to magenta. If these colour pairs enhance each other's most spellbinding qualities and energies, perhaps you could try wearing your Sun sign's lucky colour with its matching complementary colour in order to produce extra magical results! Your lucky Leonine colours are gold and orange, which are complemented respectively by indigo and blue. Now you know your colours, you can dress for success!

FEATURE COLOURS ★ GOLD & ORANGE

★ GOLD ★

"Alchemy is defined as an art of transmutation and precipitation - the changing of base metals into gold. The work of alchemical transmutation (indistinct) designated as 'the Labour of the Sun'. This 'Eye of Ra' symbolically represents the perfection with which nature is gradually unfolding in her creations. At the physical level the Sun of Perfection is represented by gold. Alchemy is the science and art which hasten the creations of Nature to attain perfection at their own respective level.

Gold is the perfection attained by metals and minerals."
Leonard Lee, *A General Look at Alchemy*

Planetary Association ★ The Sun

Complementary Colour ★ Indigo

Healing Qualities ★ Uplifting, Joyful, Playful, Bright, Transformational, Energetic, Dynamic

Keywords ★ Positive Thinking, Justice, Wealth, Nobility, Celebration, Opulence, Luxury, Prosperity, Status, Masculinity, Treasure, Perfection, Money, Rainbows

Gold is the colour of the Sun, and is used for achieving goals, overall healing, success and of course, wealth. It is associated with spiritual truths, the Divine, that which is invaluable and incorruptible, the powers of the soul, and personal attainment. The Sun is the planetary ruler of this colour and precious metal, and in Western astrology it is associated with Leo, which is also under Solar auspices. In Vedic astrology, gold is ruled by Jupiter, the planet of fortune and expansion, which links it to optimistic Sagittarius and imaginative Pisces. The shade of golden-yellow brings illumination, wisdom and wealth, for gold symbolises opulence and prosperity. Ancient people believed the Sun to be the source of all light and knowledge, and yellow came to symbolise wisdom and intellect through association.

The colour of reason, shades of golden-yellow therefore express the Solar qualities of nobility, excellence and fortune. Gold is also a colour of celebration, life-giving energy, wellbeing and plenitude, its influence bringing forth abundant harvests of everything. Gold evokes emotions and states such as youthfulness, playfulness, energy, exuberance, power, strength and joy. It is also closely connected with royalty: in mythology, everything King Midas touched turned to gold, hence the phrase 'the Midas Touch'. Alchemists and other magic workers associate gold with transformation - after all, it is the ultimate goal of alchemical processes and represents purity, perfection and enlightenment. The most commonly known magical symbol of gold is the legendary 'pot of gold at the end of the rainbow', which is symbolic of finding the ultimate treasures and therefore achieving your loftiest goal. You can connect yourself with the power of the Sun by wearing or working with gold; alternatively, gold can be used to increase the properties of other precious stones. For example, the qualities of topaz, ruby and peridot are thought to increase significantly when set in gold jewellery. Ruby in particular set in gold absorbs Solar energy and helps to revitalise the wearer.

★ ORANGE ★

"Orange is the happiest colour in the world."
Frank Sinatra

Planetary Association ★ The Sun

Complementary Colour ★ Blue

Healing Qualities ★ Success, Attraction, Antidepressant, Stimulating, Creativity, Confidence, Positivity, Laughter, Transformation, Sociability, Constructiveness

Keywords ★ Healing Powers, Playfulness, Fun, Flirtatious (red + yellow), Positive thinking, Justice, Legal Matters, Emotional Strength, Prosperity, Self Esteem, Zest, Determination, Sociability, Energy, Enthusiasm

Strong, rich, stimulating, warming and packed with positive vibrations, orange inspires achievement, joy, delight and gentle confidence. Orange has an energising vibe, promoting confidence and wellbeing. An effective antidepressant, it encourages creativity and passion, and alleviates feelings of nervousness. Orange is the symbol of feminine energy, the energy of creation. It is gentler than the dynamic energy of red, but energy-wise, they are complementary.

Combining the passion of red with the wisdom of yellow, orange is the colour of joy, zest and of dance, giving freedom to thoughts and feelings, and disperses heaviness, allowing the body natural, joyful movements. Having the ability to bring about changes in biochemical structure, orange has the capacity to disperse depression. It can be used to attract attention, signal danger and even magnetise prosperity *. Some special animals that are this colour are tigers, monarch butterflies, orang-utans (the 'people of the forest'), ginger cats and goldfish.

Orange is also a feature and predominant colour in some of nature's most spectacular sights and phenomena: sunsets, Autumn leaves, the Northern Lights, the Grand Canyon, Uluru, the ancient city of Petra and the Egyptian Pyramids to name a few. Orange is the colour of the saffron robes of Buddhism and carries with it deep insight and a profound understanding of the bliss of pure 'being', of simply living, laughing and enjoying the present moment. If you lack this simple happy vibe, orange bears the dual significance of mellow profundity and an insatiable appetite for life and living, and imparts both expansiveness and relaxation, helping you to feel more vibrant and easy going. Orange's vibratory rate is connected with the Sacral chakra, located below the navel, and is connected with physical, sexual and material desires.

Orange, as well as gold, is associated with Leo, and also the other two Fire signs, symbolising the fiery nature of these signs through such concepts as glowing embers or licking flames. It is also connected to the planet Mercury. Working with orange-coloured crystals can help bring more inspiration, self-esteem and emotional strength into your experience. Although it is generally a positive colour, avoid it if you are feeling crowded, sick, frustrated or claustrophobic. Overall, orange demands attention, exuding confidence, enthusiasm and warmth.

Gold and orange, and their respective rainbow spectrum complementary colours indigo and blue, are Leo's special LUCKY colours! These colours can be mixed and matched to dazzling and mesmerising effect

* Orange trees and their blossoms are symbols of generosity and purity. In some traditions, this tree even signifies the Tree of Knowledge of good and evil Paradise. In some magical belief systems, it is thought that placing a bowl of oranges upon a central dining table attracts wealth and prosperity into the home.

LEO'S CHAKRA CORRESPONDENCE ★ SOLAR PLEXUS

The word 'chakra' comes from the Sanskrit and means 'wheel', disc' or 'circle'. Chakras are vitally important to your physical health, emotional wellbeing and spiritual growth, and are regarded as a complete integrated system that works holistically. The chakras are funnel-shaped spinning energy vortexes of multi-coloured light. These swirling vortexes of energy absorb and distribute life-force, the subtle energy known as *prana*. The seven master chakras - Root, Sacral, Solar Plexus, Heart, Throat, Third Eye and Crown - lie in the centre line of the body, with the first five embedded within the spinal column. Each chakra vibrates at a different vibrational frequency and on a different note, and responds to specific life issues or 'thought forms'.

The lower body chakras deal with physical issues. As we move up the body, the chakras correspond to increasingly spiritual concerns. As a consequence, each chakra's energy vibrates at a different rate, depending on whether they govern earthbound or ethereal issues. The lower chakras have slower and denser vibrations, while the higher chakras spin at faster speeds with higher vibrations.

Because the chakras have no physical manifestation and cannot be located using any scientific instrument, they have tended to be viewed with scepticism by many Western medical professionals, a distinction they share with energy points in acupuncture and the notion of meridians. Instead, they are believed to have been sensed intuitively by many people over many centuries, and indeed people in yoga positions and in deep meditation have reported experiencing the sensation of a surge of energy rising from the base of the spine and emerging through the top of the head. Some people have even said they have seen points of blue light when their *kundalini* energy has risen from the lowest chakra to the highest, as well as experiencing a profound sense of happiness and ecstasy.

In summary, the Universal Life Force enters the body through the Crown chakra at the top of the head. As it works its way through the body, it flows through the other centres. As it spreads to the Base chakra, it is said to arouse the kundalini energy, which yogis believe sleeps in a coiled serpentine form.

The chakra associated with Leo is the third, or Solar Plexus chakra, which governs confidence, personal power and control.

SOLAR PLEXUS CHAKRA

Location ★ Behind the Navel
Colour ★ Yellow

Concerned with ★ Personal Power, Confidence & Control
Gland ★ Adrenals
Essential Oils ★ Chamomile, Neroli, Bergamot, Benzoin, Clary Sage, Dill, Palmarosa, Cypress, Fennel, Lemon, Hyssop, Juniper, Marjoram, Sage, Black Pepper
Animal ★ Ram
Shape ★ Downward Triangle
Element ★ Fire
Planets ★ Mars, Sun
Zodiac Signs ★ Aries, Leo
Flower ★ 10-petalled Lotus
Energy State ★ Plasma
Mantra ★ RAM

Positive Expression ★ Intelligent, optimistic, forgiving, thoughtful, perceptive

Negative Expression (Blockage) ★ Impractical, daydreaming, imbalance between the heart and head, lack of confidence, difficulty manifesting desires, low self-esteem, misuse of power, over-reliance on will, dominance, shame

The Solar Plexus chakra is located at the diaphragm. Its Sanskrit name is *manipura*, and its symbol is a ten-petal yellow lotus flower whose centre contains a red downward-pointing triangle. Balance in this chakra is expressed as self-confidence, logical thought processes and goal manifestation. It corresponds to the pancreas and the Solar nerve plexus. Crystals that can be used to cleanse and balance this chakra are mostly yellow stones, including: Citrine, Amber, Ametrine, Yellow Jasper, Amblygonite, Golden Beryl, Sunstone, Yellow Sapphire, Tiger's Eye and Yellow Tourmaline.

LUCKY CAREER TIPS & PATHS THAT WILL MAKE YOUR BANK BALANCE & SPIRITUAL SELF SOAR

The branch of astrology known as 'vocational astrology' encompasses the areas of one's calling, career path, or ideal profession. Careers, jobs, professions and occupations can all mean different things to different people, but to simplify the definition, I refer to a vocation as one's true calling, one's authentic path, and a dynamic way of life which pays an income in some form and leads to a deep fulfilment of personal and spiritual needs. An ideal vocation will provide self-fulfilment, ego satisfaction, and feed one's inner drive to achieve what they ultimately wish to achieve, whether that be to gain recognition, wealth or approval, to travel, to learn and fulfil an inner need for knowledge, an urge to serve others in some way, or an urge to improve personal, societal or Universal conditions.

In order to gain ultimate fulfilment and self-esteem, we all need a purpose in life. Many people gain this through their work, providing the job or career they choose suits their temperament, talents and aspirations. If our professional life is unsatisfactory or disharmonious in any way, frustration, unhappiness and even despair can result. Although your whole horoscope would need to be drawn up and interpreted in order to gain more substantial, deeper insights into your ideal career and purpose, you can begin by being guided by your Sun sign, which can give you many pointers to a suitable, and therefore successful, career path. You just never know, something in the following might jump out at you and make your soul dance immediately - and hopefully all the way to the bank!

With your Sun in Leo, you are a natural leader and authority figure. Leadership roles, and management and executive positions are sure to be right up your alley, as well as the creative and dramatic arts. You like to carve your own niche and give anything you do an individual touch, and your vital, gregarious nature and generosity of spirit will help you to make your own opportunities, or at least to recognise them. Your ideal vocation taps your creativity, and allows you to shine in some way, as well as to lead or rule over others.

The following fields may hold appeal: Chairman, Director, Goldsmith, Party Planner, Promotions, Youth Work, and Professional Sports.

Leos are known for their dramatism and flair for theatrics, and anything which involves display and presentation. Demonstrative and expressive, the following careers will naturally attract your Leonine spirit: Entertainer, Costume Designer, Window Display Designer, Actor, Dancer, Singer, Talk Show Host, Motivational Speaker, Circus Artist/Performer, Fashion Designer, Big Animal Trainer, Teacher, and performing for an audience in any capacity.

Leos need to express their natural exuberance and enthusiasm for life in their work, and often become deeply involved in whatever their profession is, so much so that work and leisure often become one and the same - indivisible - especially if the job allows them artistic and creative freedom, input and expression. You are one of the most likely types to mix business with pleasure, and enjoy every minute of it! In fact, your professional life may become so demanding that there is little time left for hobbies or recreation, in which case you turn your career into your play. Glamour and luxury also play a big part in your vocational life, and any field which encompasses these, such as the fashion industry and modelling, will attract you.

Being high-minded, idealistic and commanding, Leo despises amateurism in all its forms, and will always seek to work at the highest level possible. Your constant striving for betterment is admirable, and you should never find yourself in a position which stifles this quality.

Being so fixedly determined, if there is something that you set your heart upon, you will most likely achieve it and you are highly unlikely to give up until you do. Whatever it is you aim towards, always ensure that it is something which gives you the chance to demonstrate your powers of leadership and gives you the opportunity to express your creative talents.

You would make an excellent teacher, perhaps better with older children than the very young, but still, you have a flair and knack for working with all age groups and derive great satisfaction from working within spirited groups of people - young, old and everything in between; you can certainly goad them all into action!

Leos are excellent organisers and have broad vision, but cannot be bothered fussing over small details - so you need to be in a position where you can delegate the smaller bits and pieces to other people while you remain at the helm and in control. Tedium and intricacies are not your forte.

You are perhaps best suited to positions of leadership. Executive posts in all fields will appeal. You have an urge to work in occupations where you can assert your authority and 'show off' your undeniable gifts, and in this way you would make an effective top-ranking military officer, highly placed civil servant, diplomat, or almost any other eminent government post. Professions allied to high finance, stockbroking and banking are also suitable, as are principals of schools and universities. Any work entailing the use of gold will also undoubtedly lead to success for the Sun-ruled Lion.

In order to derive satisfaction from any vocation, you must eventually become one of the leaders, the person who is in a position of command or responsibility. You will never be truly happy if you have to play second fiddle or be a subordinate to others for long periods of time, and must therefore choose a professional path which offers opportunities for high levels of success, fame, recognition or wealth - and preferably *all* of the above!

In many ways, Leos make fantastic business owners, because that way you are your own boss and answerable only to yourself. But because you have such a sense of creativity, style and showmanship, you tend to shine brightest when you are around others.

When asked whether fame or fortune appeal to you more, Leos usually tend to answer 'fame'. If you can capitalise on your need and thirst for fame, glory and centre stage by honouring your spirit in the creative and dramatic arts, you will not only achieve your much-lusted-after fame, but fortune as well - as a shining, polished by-product! And isn't that what most of us strive towards?

LUCKY PLACES WHERE YOUR ENERGY IS HEIGHTENED

As the Fire element and Choleric humour corresponds with hot and dry conditions, warm, arid and low-humidity places suit your constitution, disposition and temperament. The following nations, features and cities are also places whose vibrations are closely allied with the sign of Leo: Sicily, Vanuatu, Stonehenge, Bristol, Macedonia, Puerto Rico, Columbia, Singapore, Romania, Indonesia, Switzerland, Italy (Rome), France (the Riviera), Mali, Mongolia, Seychelles, Czech Republic (Prague), Ivory Coast, Southern Iraq, Bosnia, Gabon, Malaysia, Afghanistan, Liberia, Oman, Peru, Senegal, The Congo, Burkina Faso, Bahrain, Turkey, Bohemia, Maldives, North Korea, South Korea, Lebanon, India (Mumbai) and North America (Chicago, Philadelphia). Exclusive resorts, jungles, mansions, palaces and castles are also in tune with the Leonine energy, as are places whose climate is warm and dry for the most part of the year. Any luxury adventure holiday, a road trip across Wild West America with an obligatory stop at Las Vegas and the Grand Canyon, a drive along Australia's famous Nullarbor Plain, or a desert trek on camelback (think Central Australia or Saudi Arabia), or somewhere exotic, where the climate is hot and dry (while you are there at least!) and that offers plenty of pampering, 'brag book' photo moments, and opportunities to shop, could very well be your ticket to Leonine heaven!

GEMS & CRYSTALS

"People love stones, and apparently stones love people. Like the angels they may be, they seem endlessly willing to serve the wellbeing of humans and to help us achieve our desires ...Unlike people of the ancient past, we now have access to virtually the entire mineral kingdom. We have the opportunity to work like modern alchemists, combining and arranging the stones and their currents, looking for combinations and patterns that can help us enhance our inner and outer lives."
Robert Simmons, *Stones of the New Consciousness*

Each crystal and mineral of the Earth embodies different qualities, patterns or potential expressions of the Divine language, the silent whispers of the Universe. If we can accept the fact that the human body is a sophisticated, multi-faceted antenna system comprised of a crystalline matrix that is constantly transmitting and receiving all manner of energies, it could then be assumed that energy and body workers who use quartz, shells and stones, which are also crystalline materials, have the power to promote resonant interactions with the liquid 'crystal' structures found in human tissues. It could even be said that we are all made of essentially the same substances and structures, and that crystals and gemstones vibrate at varying energetic levels which can connect with our own in order to 'buzz' and dance together to make a harmonious Uni-verse both within and without.

All crystals work through vibrational balancing and by channelling energy. The magic of crystals is in their colour, which is determined by the rate at which their atoms vibrate; these vibrations can be matched to the energy given by your own body's aura. And just as light can be focused and refracted through gemstones, so too can all kinds of psychic energy, from healing energies to Divine communications.

Gemstones can help us attune to higher vibrations and bring them into our own experience and being. This theory of crystal resonance suggests that the characteristic energy patterns emanated by any stone can be transferred into the 'liquid crystal medium' of our bodies through resonance. Our bodies, being composed of these tuneable liquids, can mimic and mirror any consistent vibrational pattern with which we come into contact; we can therefore resonate with the healthful qualities of various crystals and minerals.

Crystals and precious stones have been valued throughout world cultures over many centuries for their healing virtues and capacities to imbue courage, strength, invulnerability, clairvoyance, love and numerous other qualities. Wearing gemstones is one of the simplest and most effective self-healing practices you can undertake, and wearing or carrying those stones whose vibrations correspond with the qualities you wish to embody brings their energetic currents into engagement with your body.

Over time the phenomenon of energetic integration, may be felt tangibly and your own vibrational field may internalise the stone's currents and adjust to them and effectively 'store' them, making them, eventually, a part of your own vibrational make-up. And we seem to know from the resonances we feel within our bodies when in contact with these gemstones, that crystals emanate tangible, if oft immeasurable, currents.

Crystals act as transmitters and amplifiers of your will or intentions - as long as your will or intentions are in sympathy with the crystal's energy. The mineral kingdom refers to stones, minerals and crystals and the associations and vibrations they carry. When working with stones, we are working with several different layers of spiritual energies, and although they can be regarded as inanimate 'psychic batteries', they are actually moving, vibrating masses of energy which transmit potential and power into our lives. Some crystals and stones even have receptive powers, which means they can absorb energy and retain it within until cleansed or re-programmed.

Although it is untrue that the only stones you can usefully wear are the ones astrologically matched with your Sun sign or ruling planet, those which align with your Sun sign or ruling planet are your most fortuitous and therefore strongest 'attractors' and 'amplifiers'.

Twelve oracular gemstones were described in the Bible, as the author of *Exodus* (28-15 and 17-21) knew them. Yahweh spoke to Moses about the breastplate he would have to wear to train for priesthood, and described it to him in these words: "And thou shalt make the breastplate of judgement with cunning work; ... And thou shalt set in it settings of stones, even four rows of stones; the first row shall be a sardius, a topaz, and a carbuncle. And the second row shall be an emerald, a sapphire and a diamond. And the third row an opal, an agate and an amethyst. And the fourth row a beryl, and an onyx, and a jasper; they shall be set in hold in their inclosings. And the stones shall be with the children … (all) twelve (of them)." Given that the compilers of the Bible lived during a time when astrological belief was prevalent in Babylon, it seems valid to assert that these previously named gemstones would have some astrological basis. Further, since these ancient people supposedly made correlations between each of the twelve precious stones, and one of the twelve zodiac signs, there are seven crystalline systems set down in crystallography (or the science of the laws which influence the formation, structure and geometric, physical and chemical properties of crystallised matter) as analogous with the seven traditional ruling planets of the zodiac.

However, nobody is under the rule of one planet alone. We are all in essence a complex mixture of every planet, many elements and varying aspects, depending on their positions, placements and prominence in our birth chart. Everything that goes on in the skies above us affects what is going on here on Earth, and also *within* us. Your lucky stones are to assist you to tune into your Sun sign's energy and planetary influences, but you are by no means limited to the ones listed for your sign alone. Above all, let your stones, whichever ones you choose, work for you and allow them to transport your very own unique and magical energy into the wider Universe.

"Beautiful and strong is the material of stones, but more beautiful and much more powerful is the mystery that emanates from them."
Chinese Poet & Alchemist, Li Po, 8th Century A.D.

★ CLEAR QUARTZ ★

The Master Healer ★ *For All Zodiac Signs*

A common, well-known and popular gem, clear quartz (sometimes known as rock crystal) is an all-purpose 'jack-of-all-trades' stone. It amplifies the magic of any work you do or wishes you make. It is connected with all the chakras and increases the power of all other crystals. Clear quartz is a deep soul cleanser, which unblocks and regulates energy and emotions on all levels. It is balancing and harmonising. In various cultures, quartz crystal is reputed to be the most powerful crystal, the 'grandfather crystal', and the 'chief of the Stone People'. Clear quartz is also considered to be the only gemstone that is modifiable to suit your needs *, as other crystals automatically contain and retain their own specific resonance or natural signature. In essence, clear quartz is the most easily programmable and the most overall healing and readily accessible crystals of the mineral kingdom, holding a unique importance in the Universe of gems. And because of its all-encompassing nature and wide-ranging healing abilities, it has zodiacal affinities with all the signs.

* To program your clear quartz crystal, simply hold it on your Third Eye chakra (between and just above the

physical eyes) and concentrate on the purpose for which you wish to use it. Be positive and receptive while you allow your crystal to fill with this energy. If you wish, you could also state the intention of the programming out loud, for example, 'I program this crystal for love / healing / meditation / abundance / protection or (insert your own word here)'. You could also run your clear quartz crystal under running water, allow it to dry naturally, then hold the stone with both hands, bring it up to your mouth and blow into it sharply three times in order to impregnate it with your own breath. Then, hold it firmly in one hand and silently invite and welcome it into your life as a friend, helper and guide.

LEONINE & SOLAR LUCKY CRYSTALS, STONES & GEMS

Leo birth stones ★ Citrine, Ruby, Peridot

July birth stones ★ Onyx, Turquoise, Ruby, Carnelian

August birth stones ★ Carnelian, Moonstone, Peridot, Sardonyx

Citrine, Ruby, Peridot (your three primary birthstones), Onyx, Turquoise, Carnelian, Moonstone and Sardonyx (July and August birth stones) are your luckiest stones, and one or more of these gems should be worn about your person to ensure good luck and increase your magnetism. Boji Stone, Fire Agate, Diamond, Amber, Chrysolite, Cat's Eye, Golden Beryl, Yellow Spinel, Garnet, Chrysocolla, Tiger's Eye, Kunzite, Sunstone, Emerald, Green and

Pink Tourmaline, Orange Calcite, Yellow Calcite, Larimar, Petalite, Clear Quartz, Tibetan Quartz, Pyrite, Labradorite, Titanium Quartz, Yellow Sapphire, Aqua Aura, Red Obsidian, Golden Topaz, Heliodor, Rhodochrosite, and all yellow/orange stones also align with Leonine energy. To bring about even greater luck these stones should be set in gold, since this is the metal of the Sun, ruler of Leo.

CRYSTALS & THE PLANETS

All the Vedic texts agree in relating gems to planets. This verse from the *Jatax Parijat* links each gem to a planet:

'The ruby is the gem of the Lord of the Day (the Sun),
The shining pearl is the gem of the cold Moon,
Red coral is the gem of Mars,
The emerald is the gem of noble Mercury,
Yellow sapphire is the gem of Jupiter, instructor of gods,
Diamond is the gem of Venus, instructor of demons,
Blue sapphire is the gem of Saturn.'

Each planet influences its gem, and their curative power varies according to the position of its planet in the zodiac. Ayurvedic medicine has always paid attention to these details in their healing practices, often advising people to wear their corresponding zodiacal stone as a ring or a talisman.

CRYSTALS & THE ELEMENTS

Crystals are inextricably linked to the four elements, from their original creation to their potency and use in magical rituals and healing. Formed by the combination, in varying conditions, of different physical elements, such as metals, non-metals and gases, some stones require the enormous heat generated by volcanoes or deep thermal currents to bond their molecular makeup, while others may require pressure or water sources. The effects of the four elements of Fire, Earth, Air and Water is evident in these formation processes. The heat generated by Fire, pressure from the Earth, and the chemical reactions involved in absorbing elements from the Air and Water, all demonstrate the four elements in action to produce the correct conditions and ingredients necessary for the creation of crystals, lending them each their unique qualities.

CRYSTALS & THE FIRE ELEMENT

The transformational influence of Fire can be seen in such examples as citrine, which is formed when heat is applied to amethyst, and obsidian, which is created through astonishing volcanic temperatures. Although Fire can be a destructive force, its effect is also to change things, and it is this transformative energy which can be harnessed in Fire-inspired gemstones to help facilitate positive changes in your life, through meditation, chakra balancing or other magical rituals.

Some Fiery crystals are ★ Calcite, Ruby, Amber, Obsidian, Garnet, Citrine, Bloodstone (Heliotrope), Topaz, Spinel and Pyrite.

THE CRYSTALLINE SYSTEM OF YOUR RULING BODY THE SUN

Associated with your ruler the Sun, are Amber, Chrysolite, Diamond, Onyx, Ruby, Topaz and Fluorite. These belong to the crystalline system known as cubic, which is a cubic shape as the name suggests. The stone most representative of this system is Fluorite, which in ancient times was reputed to strengthen thinking, the powers of concentration and reflection, and to bring peace and calm to the minds of those who wore it.

THE SUN'S GEMSTONE ASSOCIATION

★ **RUBY** ★ Ruby derives its name from the Latin *rubens* or *rubeus*, meaning 'red'. A variety of the mineral corundum, it has a hardness of 9. Because it symbolised happiness and brightness, and was believed to be the most beautiful of gems, it came to be associated with the sign of Leo. This association was also made because of its power in bringing success, wealth and joy, and because its symbolic virtues included courage, nobility, spirit and loyalty. The ancients considered ruby to be the stone of the Sun and believed it represented the life force and fire. The gem of northern summer, ruby burns with a captivating fire. Ruby has long been regarded as a symbol of love, beauty, passion, success, strength, protection and power. It aids in strengthening and refining the natural abilities you were born with. It is a stone of immense power and vitality, and can be worn to stimulate pure life force energy. Its spirit is a great ally to those who wish to work magic in their lives. Imparting vigour to your journey, it energises and balances but may sometimes overstimulate more delicate or irritable types. Ruby encourages the setting of realistic goals, improves motivation and stimulates passion for living. It stimulates the Heart chakra and enlivens the heart, encouraging you to 'follow your bliss'. It is also a powerful energiser for the Base chakra. Ruby signifies and arouses lust, and governs the sexual and reproductive organs. It can be used to release any energy blockages deep within the self, and to activate, vitalise, intensify and increase desire. It utilises infrared, the slowest vibration of the colour spectrum, giving a new boost to processes that have been sluggish or stagnant.

Ruby is one of the stones of abundance and aids in retaining wealth and a healthy, driven passion. Ruby brings up anger or negative energy, transmutes them, and removes anything unfavourable from your path. Promoting lively leadership and confidence, ruby brings about a positive and courageous state of mind. Essentially, ruby is a dynamic stone which charges up passion, banishes sadness, warns of danger or imminent misfortune (by darkening in colour), attracts sexual activity, fires up enthusiasm, and helps one overcome exhaustion, apathy and lethargy by imparting potency and vigour. It can stop outside forces from draining your energy. Ruby renews one's passion for life, truth, courage, wisdom and perseverance, emitting an abundance of cheerfulness.

LEO'S FEATURE CRYSTAL ★ CITRINE

Citrine is known in crystal healing circles as the success, prosperity, abundance and happiness stone, and is an attractive, bright, golden-yellow gem that takes its name from the old French word 'citron', meaning 'lemon' or 'yellow'. The golden-yellow colour of citrine quartz is formed when high temperatures are applied to amethyst or smoky quartz. Citrine carries the power of your ruler the Sun, and has a particular affinity with the Solar Plexus chakra. Its beneficial energies also work well with the Sacral and Heart chakras. It is associated with good fortune, luck, abundance, manifestation, and increases personal power and energy. Citrine is an exceedingly beneficial stone, a powerful cleanser and regenerator, is warming, energising and highly creative. This is a willpower stone, being connected to the Sun, and is particularly helpful for helping to release old patterns of behaviours or thoughts that stand in the way of our achieving greatness.

Being so highly Solar in nature, citrine energises every level of life, promotes clarity and puts us in touch with celestial Fire and the powers of our brightest luminary and the core essence of our self - the Sun; in this way, it can help to raise self-esteem and self-confidence. Because it is a stone of positivity, it dispels destructive tendencies, improves motivation, encourages self-expression, activates individuality and enhances creativity; in fact, it is excellent for dissolving blockages to creativity. Further, it is useful for overcoming depression, fears and phobias, and promotes the inner calm that enables wisdom to emerge. Citrine awakens the higher mind, stimulates inspiration and frees the mind of limitations, helping to turn ideas into reality. It amplifies and regenerates energy, and being the product of heat-treated amethyst or smoky quartz, it carries the forces of transmutation and inner alchemy.

Its bright yellow colour is literally like a sunbeam shining into your life, helping you to gain insight or confidence when you need to manifest change. This stone helps you look forward optimistically to the future instead of hanging onto the past; it also promotes exploration and enjoyment of new experiences. It is an aura protector and has the ability to cleanse the chakras, especially the Solar Plexus and Sacral chakras. But it also activates the Crown chakra, opens the intuition and balances the subtle bodies, aligning them with the physical. It is a good stone to use if you wish to develop your psychic abilities, especially if you have problems trusting and acting on your instincts. Hold a piece of citrine in your hand when you are undertaking any psychic work, such as mediumship or scrying, and it will enhance your inspiration and reasoning capacities. Citrine is one of the stones of abundance. This dynamic stone teaches how to attract, manifest and keep wealth, prosperity and success. Citrine has the power to impart joy to all who behold it, and overall it promotes joy in life. It is a happy, generous stone that encourages wonder, enthusiasm and delight, filling any dark areas with cheer and light. Citrine's wonderful nature means that it can enliven you and connect you strongly with the light of your inner being. Working with this stone will help you instinctively 'put out there' what you most wish to attract. Transmuting energy and radiating positivity, and holding the energy of wealth, keep this stone in your cashbox or purse to attract prosperity. It is interesting to note that this stone never needs cleansing.

LEONINE POWER CRYSTALS

Around six thousand years ago, in ancient Mesopotamia, the Sumerians started studying precious stones and minerals, as well as the stars, with a view of improving their lives in many ways by probing the secrets and mysteries of the Universe. Their esoteric interests and knowledge were such that they began to grasp the general connections between the Earth and the heavens, or the Solar system as they knew it, and the functions of stones and minerals as a link between the two. Their method of making these connections was by colour (for example the Sun was allocated all yellow stones), as well as other spiritual links. The gemstones listed for the portion of your zodiac sign are given their status as your 'power crystals' due to the links that can be made between your primary planetary ruler/s and your mutable planetary ruler (listed last), and each stone's particular colour, chemical and mineral compositions, healing properties, and the number they are given (based on the Mohs scale of hardness: for example, diamond scores a perfect 10 out of 10), all of which combine to align with your planetary rulers. Working mindfully with your planet's special crystals is one way you can increase the flow of power and magic into your life.

POWER CRYSTALS FOR FIRST HALF LEONINES ★ (22 July - 5 August)

Influenced by the Sun and Jupiter
Yellow Diamond, Zircon, Phenacite, Vanadinite, Muscovite

★ **ZIRCON** ★ Zircon takes its name from the Persian word 'zargun' meaning 'golden' or 'all shades of yellow', and has long been used as an amulet and talisman. This many-coloured, transparent gem should never be underestimated either as a jewel or as a holistic healing tool. Thought by the Ancient Greeks to strengthen the mind and bring joy to the heart, zircon once took precedence over almost all gemstones on account of its lustre and beautiful reflection of light. It comes in varieties from colourless to shades of yellow, light green and brown (also called jacinth, hyacinth and malacon), and blue and red (heat-treated only). In any shade, its brilliance is often equal to that of diamond. Although similar to the diamond in its lustre and light, the zircon is less authoritarian in character but still firm in its direct beneficial actions on physical and psychological states of being. Zircon holds within itself the essence of the Sun and Jupiter, which carry the energy of existence and the life-force. The overriding characteristic of this crystal is its vitality, which acts with effectiveness on both physical and mental disorders. On the spiritual plane, it promotes self-development and facilitates the expansion of the higher mind. In ancient times, zircon was regarded as a mind tonic that prevented thoughts from straying and maintained a person's focus. It can therefore be used to boost concentration during meditation and can aid chakra work and other modes of spiritual healing. Zircon is thought to contain 'decisive' powers and is a useful stone to use when wishing to take control of a situation and overcome indecision. It strengthens one's resolve and if you are at a low ebb, it picks you up, energises you, improves your outlook, and re-attunes you to your outer environment. The positive properties of this stone are enhanced by the Sun, so charging zircon with sunlight can be an effective way of increasing its powers. An uplifting stone, zircon can help you find your inner strength, lift melancholy, tap into your potential, and release your fear of failure.

★ **PHENACITE** ★ Phenacite is a rare mineral which often crystallises in short prisms, with a hardness of 7.5 to 8. A great Third Eye awakener, phenacite is a supreme stone of spirituality, its pulsing energies felt at the Third Eye even by people not normally sensitive to crystal energies. This stimulation is stronger than one can receive from virtually any other stone. It can also be used to awaken the latent special capacities residing in the prefrontal lobes, the newest and most advanced region of the human brain, sometimes bringing spontaneous experiences of telepathy, psychokinesis, remote viewing (intuitively sensing faraway situations), or prophetic visions. Phenacite's link with the higher realms make it a powerful tool for the manifestation of inner images or patterns of intention in the outer physical world. In fact, it is highly recommended that this stone be used in combination with yellow sapphire and/or cinnabar quartz to attract financial abundance and prosperity.

★ **VANADINITE** ★ Sun-ruled Leos with Jupiter as their mutable body have this brilliant orange, brown, red or a combination of all three colours, mineral as their unusual power crystal. Belonging to the lead family, and rich in vanadium, a grey metallic element used for strengthening steel, Vanadinite is comprised of out-of-the-ordinary, complex chemicals. Dazzlingly beautiful and tougher than steel, vanadinite crystals usually grow on dark, worn-looking rock, generously filling crevices and coating the outside with smaller, lighter coloured sunset-toned crystals. Vanadinite has a strong connection with the Earth chakra, which sits in the Earth body beneath the feet. It is therefore a useful crystal for people who have problems accepting their physicality, as it grounds the soul into the physical body and helps it to feel comfortable in the Earth realm. Mentally, vanadinite fills the gap between the intellect and thought, allowing insight and rational thought to combine in an inner voice of guidance. It also assists in defining and pursuing one's goals by shutting out unwanted mind clutter and inducing a state of 'no mind' so that one can be more focused on visions and journeying. Psychologically it helps to facilitate deep inner peace by closing out mental noise, clearing the mind, and opening up an internal channel within the body to receive a flow of Universal energy. Vanadinite can also help to curb overspending and when placed in the wealth corner or in your purse, it is believed to help you retain your money.

★ **MUSCOVITE** ★ A pearly, shimmering mineral, Muscovite is also known as mica, and is the commonest form of it. Coming in shades of pink, green, brown, grey, violet, red, white and yellow, muscovite is a mystical and visionary stone with strong angelic connections (particularly the pink-hued variety) and links to the higher self (particularly the violet-hued variety). It facilitates astral travel and opens up the intuitive and psychic functions. Used in scrying, or crystal gazing, this stone can stimulate contact with the highest spiritual realms. Aligning with the Heart chakra, it allows recognition of humanity's flaws but stimulates a flow of unconditional love and acceptance. Psychologically, muscovite helps to dissolve and disperse confusion, self-doubt and insecurity. Being a spiritually reflective crystal, it is also useful in helping you to see yourself as others see you, helping to integrate and transform the qualities you do not necessarily like about yourself. It assists this process further by supporting you during the exploration of any painful feelings which may be evoked, and aids in changing the image you present to the outside world. Stimulating quick-wittedness and problem-solving capacities, muscovite facilitates clearer expression of thoughts and feelings, making you an overall more effective person. Muscovite is also believed to improve your appearance, by imparting sheen to the hair and a sparkle to the eyes.

POWER CRYSTALS FOR SECOND HALF LEONINES ★ (6 - 21 August)

White Diamond, Heliodor, Sphene, Sulphur, 'Volcanic Bombs'

★ **WHITE DIAMOND** ★ Diamond is pure crystallised carbon and is known as the ruler of the mineral kingdom, due to its hardwearing qualities, hardness and sheer brilliance. Diamond is the purest substance in nature and one of the hardest (10 out of 10 on the Mohs scale). The word 'diamond' has its origin in the Greek word 'adamas', which means unconquerable. Mined for over 4,000 years, ancient civilisations discovered that this amazing gem could cut any other stone. The diamond is known universally as a token of love; quite simply, it is the ultimate symbol of purity. This luminously brilliant gem, through its renowned purity and durability, offers incomparable proof of total perfection expressed in a single element. Its pure white light can help to bring your life into a cohesive whole, the first step in using your power to optimum effect. It bonds relationships, is said to enhance the love of a husband to his wife, brings love and clarity into a partnership, and is seen as a sign of commitment and faithfulness. Psychologically, this precious gem imparts a sense of fearlessness, fortitude and invincibility, for diamonds are unbreakable in every sense of the word. Diamond is also an amplifier of any energy with which it comes into contact, therefore should only be used for positive spells and magic, and is one of the few stones that never needs recharging or cleansing; in fact, it increases the energy of whatever it comes into contact with and is very effective when used with other crystals for healing as it enhances and draws out their power. Like the clear quartz, it is a master healer which accelerates the spiritual development of its wearer. As an amplifier of energy, the merciless light of diamond will highlight anything that is negative and requires transformation. Diamond has been a symbol for wealth for thousands of years and is one of the stones of manifestation, with the ability to attract abundance; the larger the diamond, the more abundance will be drawn to the requester. Diamond helps to clear emotional and mental pain, alleviates fear and brings about new beginnings. It also provides a link between the intellect and the higher mind, aiding clarity and enlightenment of mind. On a spiritual level, it allows one's soul light to shine out, cleansing the aura of anything shrouding the inner light, and reminds you of your soul's aspirations; it activates the Crown chakra, linking it to the 'Divine light'. Indeed, clear crystals such as diamond will interact with your energy field by raising your vibration through clearing away any cloudiness or blockages within your subtle bodies. Diamond is overall a highly creative stone, stimulating imagination and inventiveness, and aiding spiritual evolution.

★ **HELIODOR** ★ Golden-hued heliodor is a type of beryl which forms through extreme pressure and high temperatures. Heliodor, or golden beryl as it is also known, heals stress in the mental body by activating and integrating the Crown and Solar Plexus chakras. It opens gateways to our understanding of archetypal realms, and by giving you this greater insight into the role you are playing in your life drama, it allows you to step out of the illusion to view your true situation more clearly, which in turn promotes greater psychological and emotional stability. It consoles, rejuvenates and achieves its powerful effects through its ability to reconcile the conscious and the unconscious mind. Although it works essentially through the Solar Plexus, it actually relates to the circulatory system and the heart, where it operates to energise the inner self and the intellect - and indeed, to link the two. Also, by expanding your Crown chakra to bring in higher guidance, it allows your Solar Plexus chakra to shine with more clarity and the essence of the Sun. The expanded self-awareness that results will facilitate the broadening of perspective where false judgments and delusions about yourself and others can be released. Often showing radioactivity and generally thought to be tinted by iron, both of which are emitted by the Sun, heliodor resembles a solid chunk of golden light, and in healing radiates a corresponding warmth. This lemon to rich-yellow transparent power crystal has the potential to be a medium of great spiritual illumination.

★**VOLCANIC BOMBS** ★ Volcanic bombs resemble small, blackish pears and, while not pretty, are certainly fascinating. Measuring only a few millimetres in diameter, volcanic bombs originated as molten rock spewed out from a volcano. While still 'fluid' these pellets spun in flight, and in the process gradually solidified into spindle-shaped, solid minerals.

YOUR LUCKY NUMBERS

Your lucky numbers are ★ 5 for Leo ^ & 1 for the Sun (also, see 'Lucky Magic Square of the Sun')

LUCKY MAGIC SQUARE OF THE SUN

In Western occult tradition, each planet has traditionally been associated with a series of numbers and particular arrangements of those numbers. One such method of numerological organisation is the magic square. Magic squares date back to ancient times, appearing in China about 3,000 years ago. The first Chinese square is seen in the scroll of the river Lo - the Lo-Shu, a scroll believed to have been created by Fuh-Hi, the mythical founder of Chinese civilisation. Certain squares came to be linked with the planets; these associations came from the Babylonians. Each *kamea*, or magic square, is linked with a particular planet, and each of the squares has a *seal*, which is the geometric pattern created by following the numbers in order of their value. This pattern touches upon all the numbers of the square and the seal is used to represent the entire square. An intelligence and a spirit are also associated with each kamea, derived from the key numbers contained within it, using a Hebrew form of numerology. This intelligence is viewed as an inspiring, guiding and informing entity.

The 'Magic Square of the Sun' is divided into 36 cells, or squares, six across and six down. The sum of the numbers in the vertical, horizontal and diagonal lines is a constant of 111. The total of these numbers is 666. Therefore, the numbers 6, 36, 111 and 666 are also assigned to the Sun.

YOUR NUMEROLOGY NUMBER & LUCKY SUN SIGN NUMBERS

"Everything that exists has a vibration. The vibration of sound, music, colour, matter, even our words, thoughts, and names show form. All vibration is measurable. To measure we need numbers. Numbers are the basis of all. Numbers are the key to all mysteries."
Shirley Blackwell Lawrence, *Behind Numerology*

Numerology is essentially the metaphysical * 'science' of numbers. The use of numbers in magic is its cornerstone of power. The ancient Greek philosopher and mathematician Pythagoras, born around 590 BC, embarked on a thirty-year spiritual quest studying with important religious and esoteric teachers and healers to find the mystery of 'The Hidden Light', and came to see mankind as living in three worlds: the natural, the human and the Divine. He asserted that all things can be expressed in numerical terms, because they are ultimately reducible to numbers. Pythagoras stated that "Numbers are the first things of all of Nature" and followed the theory that "Nothing can exist without numbers."

Many believe that numbers have an arcane, mystical relationship with words, and with inanimate and animate objects; the interpretations that arose from these relationships date back to a time when the dawning intelligence of primitive man first visualised the meaning of numbers and associated it with spiritual significance. Numerology is the science of the exploration of this relationship in order to discover hidden meanings, forecast the future or interpret the character of a person. In its more modern applications, a series of figures which correspond to an individual's name and date of birth are calculated, and practitioners believe one's prospects, fortune and character can be deciphered from the results ^.

So what is numerology and how does one use it? Everything in the Universe has a vibrational frequency, an energy, a force, all vibrating at various rates, and we as humans are no exception, the difference between one person and another is their rate of vibration. This force or energy is constantly in motion and changing, and we can even 'tune into' and feel our vibrations if we are still for long enough.

Along with letters, sounds, colours, crystals, and many other things, it is believed that numbers also have vibrations, and when we are able to familiarise ourselves with our own numerical frequencies, we can use this familiarity to add power and magic to our lives. The numbers of our birth date, the letters of our names, and the numbers of our Sun sign and ruling planets, all have a unique vibrational frequency, and herein lies the key to understanding our self and our journey through life. Numerology refers to the knowledge contained within the numbers of our birth date and our name, and this is our own personal magic which can greatly assist us through life.

* Metaphysics is the study of those sciences that extend beyond the physical or tangible

HOW TO FIND YOUR NUMEROLOGY NUMBER

^ Your Sun sign's number was added up according to the principle of corresponding a number with a letter, for example 1=A, 2=B, 3=C and so on in sequence and up to 9=I, then beginning again at number 1 for the next letter J and following this same sequence. Following this system, the sum of the letters in Leo vibrates to the number 5.

Your personal numerology number is determined by adding up all the numbers in your birth date until they reach a two-digit figure. The two resulting numbers are then added together again to form a single digit, which is your personal numerology number. For example, someone born on 3 February 1983, would add the digits 3 + 2 + 1 + 9 + 8 + 3 = 26 = (reduced to two digits) 8. So that person's personal numerology birth number is 8.

Each primary number or birth number from 1 to 9 has a specific meaning and is governed by a planetary force. The principle of numerology reduces all numbers down to the following: 1 to 9, and 10, 11, 13 and 22 *. The last four numbers only apply to people specially concerned with the occult and spiritualism - and can be studied at greater length through other sources if so desired - and can in any case be reduced further to a single digit if preferred. Your birth number contains a unique power, and therein lie your strengths, shortcomings and opportunities. It is beyond the scope of this book to outline your individual numerology number possibilities, so for the purposes of astrological applications, I have only included your Sun sign and ruling planet's special numbers.

* The numbers 10 and 13, and the master numbers 11 and 22, can be further reduced to one digit if so desired; however, they can be interpreted as they are without further reduction. The choice is personal.

BASIC MEANINGS & KEYWORDS

1 ★ Sun. Masculine influence, beginnings, independence, inventiveness, originality, leadership, exploration, innovation, ambition
2 ★ Moon. Feminine influence, cooperation, partnership, tact, diplomacy, harmony, unity, emotions, imagination, adaptability
3 ★ Jupiter. Communication, expression, youthfulness, self-confidence, creativity, inspiration, optimism, curiosity
4 ★ Uranus. Order, form, security, stability, patience, restriction, work, values, practicality
5 ★ Mercury. Freedom, inconsistency, change, variety, travel, activity, learned
6 ★ Venus. Love, home, family, sense of duty, responsibility, marriage, justice, nurturing, balance, gentleness, peace, friendship
7 ★ Neptune. Analysis, wisdom, mystical, spiritual, solitude, precision, research, integrity, mystery, psychic perceptions.

8 ★ Saturn. Money, power, success, organisation, hard work, business, health, purpose, control, authority, mastery

9 ★ Mars. Completion, endings, Universal, service, humanity, philanthropy, loyalty

10 ★ Fortunate, creative, vibrant, stable, optimistic, original, successful, determined, individualistic

11 ★ Master number. Prophecies, inspiration, moral courage, missionary, long-suffering, foolhardiness, enlightenment, invention

13 ★ Misunderstood, fearful, changeable, interested in the occult, fatalistic, flexible, sacred, beguiling

22 ★ Master number. Powerful, successful, idealistic, attracted to the occult, creative, wise, successful, masterful, spiritually understanding

★ THE NUMBER 1 - FOR THE SUN ★

Names ★ Monad, Unity, Whole

Arithmomantic connections with the letters of the alphabet ★ A, J and S

Ruled by the Sun, number 1, which is truly indivisible, signifies power, stoutness of heart, independence, action and responsibility. A very powerful number, it represents unity and wholeness. It is the first masculine number and the number of beginnings, and is therefore considered to be the number of the Universe and the highest order. Symbolising the Sun and Leo, its colours are yellow, orange and gold. The number 1 stands for all that is strong, individual, original, protective and creative.

This is a powerful number and it augurs success; woe betide anyone who dares to threaten those ruled by this mighty number! One is a strong vibration and indicates the ability to stand alone. As it is governed by the life-force of the Sun, it stands for independence, the development of ideas and the courage to follow them through. It also represents the ego and selfishness so lessons concerning those issues will probably arise, for the betterment of the person. It is a perfect number for those who want to run their own show in some way, and for those who wish to get ahead.

People who have 1 as a birth number tend to be leaders, not followers, and may sometimes be overbearing, impatient, stubborn, arrogant and intolerant. Number 1s love to champion causes and, like all great visionaries, tend to need a host of minions to clean up after them. The number of innovators and winners, but also tyrants, number 1 people are born leaders, ambitious and active, and well as often dominant and aggressive. Those who come under the influence of the Monad (Unity, as expressed by the figure 1) will show great tenacity and singleness of purpose. This indicates self-reliance, an unswerving desire for action, resolve, ingenuity, concentration, great achievement and possibly even genius. You can be implicitly relied upon, as you seem to take pleasure in the assumption of great responsibilities. Number 1 people can be very self-centred and ruthless if crossed, and your chosen career or calling will probably receive more energy and attention than your personal relationships. You will not be content to lead an aimless, subordinate life, but rather will seek new and sometimes hazardous paths which lead you onwards and ever upwards, towards your goals or aims. Usually you will be friendly and considerate to others, and will do all you can to assist those in need or distress.

You are independent, ambitious, self-assured, determined, individualistic, driven, focused, initiating, progressive, strong-willed, courageous, and constructively rebellious. If you were born under the influence of the number 1, you can be intolerant, narrow-minded and above receiving the advice from friends. Although you are the innovators and ideas people, and love to try new things, you are not very good at sharing yourself. To bring the best out in your personality, you should attempt to temper your rampant your self-confidence and be more willing to embrace and accept the opinions of older and more experienced people. Sunday is your special day.

Alchemy ★ Oneness preserves the integrity of creation, and cannot be divided without losing its integrity. Alchemists talk about one truth, one matter, one process: "One is the All, and by it the All, and in it the All, and if it does not contain the All it is nothing." It is usually represented as a point or circle. Finally, there is the monad, considered by the Renaissance alchemists, philosophers and esoteric practitioners to be the great, unifying principle and soul of the world.

LUCKY 'MAGIC HOURS' OR 'TIME UNITS'

One rule of magic, luck and power, as already outlined elsewhere in this book, can be found within the well-known phrase, "As above, so below." From the most ancient times, the planets were said to rule Earthly destinies and powers. Days of the week were named after the seven planets which were the only ones then known: Sun Day, Moon Day, Mars Day (French: Mardi), Mercury Day (French: Mercredi), Jove Day (French: Jeudi), Venus Day (French: Vendredi) and Saturn Day.

The planetary hours are based on an ancient astrological system, the Chaldean order of the planets. The Chaldean order indicates the relative orbital velocity of the planets, and from a heliocentric (Helios = The Sun) perspective, this sequence also indicates the relative distance of the planets from the Sun (the Sun switching places with the Earth in this sequence), and the distance of the Moon from the Earth.

Before an action is taken in daily life, or a transaction undertaken, for instance, it is possible to choose the appropriate day and hour that will provide the greatest chances of success. By studying the planetary hours system, you will discover which actions are propitious to which of the seven planets or 'star-gods' and at what time it would be advisable to undertake them.

The planetary hours system uses this Chaldean order to divide time, and each planetary hour of the planetary day is ruled by a different planet. The order is repeated, starting with the slowest: Saturn - then, Jupiter, Mars, Sun, Venus, Mercury, Moon, then back to Saturn, Jupiter, Mars, etc., ad infinitum. The planet that rules the first hour of the day is also the ruler of that whole day and gives the day its name. So the first hour of Saturday is ruled by Saturn, the first hour of Sunday by the Sun, and so on. It is important, for the purposes of using specific planetary energies for our magic and wishes, to note that planetary hours are not considered the same length as our normal time-keeping slots of sixty minutes. Each day is split into time periods, day time and night time, beginning at around sunrise and sunset respectively. These two time periods are each divided into twelve equal-length hours, which are the planetary hours. So the planetary hours of the day and the planetary hours of the night will be of different lengths, except during the equinoxes when light and darkness are balanced.

In sequence, the Sun, Moon and the five visible planets each exerts its own special influence over a twenty-four-hour period. I like to call your planet's special day and hour the 'Magic Hour'.

Magic rituals to draw luck and love to you should be conducted at astrologically correct times and with the appropriate instruments, tools, cards, herbs, flowers, oils and plants which are linked with the ruling planet. For example, a love ritual, spell or potion demands a concoction of any or all of the above ruled by Venus. Do not underestimate rulerships, for they wield an unseen power that can help make our dreams, big and small, come true.

Further, as specific hours of each day are ruled by certain planets, if you are really serious about attracting some power, luck or magic into your life, it is imperative that you wish, pray or ask at the most opportune times for your Sun sign. There are two methods you can use for fine tuning your magical workings. The first method is to perform your spell, ritual or wishing on the day your Sun sign's ruling planet during the planetary hour that signifies the essence of what you are asking for (e.g. A Leo who is looking for love might perform a love-seeking ritual on a Sunday, during a Venus-ruled planetary hour). Alternatively, if you wish to summon the power of your Sun sign's own ruling planet, then that same Leo might perform their love-seeking ritual on a Friday (ruled by Venus) during the Sun's planetary hour.

The nature of that which you are asking for, such as love, travel opportunities, money, career guidance, protection or friendship for example, should always be considered when choosing the day or hour during which your magic will be heightened.

The answer to the question why are there seven days in a week, is a very important one to know in unravelling the secret of your Magic Hours. Ancient people recognised the supreme importance of the seven heavenly spheres, which comprised those which could be seen by the naked eye: The Sun, Moon, Mercury, Venus, Mars, Jupiter and Saturn. They then named each of the seven days of the week after one of those spheres and assigned that planetary 'ruler' to one day of the week. As viewed from Earth, these seven spheres appear to move at varying speeds, and the ancients used this factor to arrange them in order of varying speed. If you intend to use your Magic Hours to attract wonderful things, you must memorise that sequence because it is what forms the basis of the whole system.

Whenever you intend to use your Magic Hours or, perhaps more accurately, Magic *Time Units*, it is important to find out the exact time of sunrise for the area in which you live, as sunrise marks the time when your planet's magic is at its most powerful on its specific day. So, at sunrise on Sunday, the Sun rules the hour following the sunrise, the Moon rules the first hour following sunrise on a Monday, and through the week the pattern is repeated, with each day's ruling planet beginning the cycle in that first hour after dawn. It is logical then, that the rest of the planets, in sequence, follow on with one planet per hour for that day thereafter for the rest of the 24-hour cycle, creating a Magic Hour or Time Unit for each planet throughout the day and night, depending on which planet rules that particular day and is therefore the first in line.

If you wish to explore the idea in more depth, it is worth noting first and foremost that each day contains twenty-four hours, but, depending on the season, day and night will be of varying lengths. In summer, daylight is longer than darkness, whereas the reverse applies in winter. During autumn and spring, day and night are usually about equal. Therefore, although a complete day always contains twenty-four hours, there are not always twelve hours between sunrise and sunset and another twelve hours between sundown and the following sunrise. So, depending on the season (and location), a time unit may be shorter than one hour, longer than one hour, or equal to one hour. So whenever you intend to use your Magic Time Units, it is important to find out the exact time of sunrise and sunset for the area in which you live. The next step is to divide the amount of day time (if day when you wish to work your 'magic', otherwise the same following theory applies to night time) into twelve equal sections by calculating the number of hours and minutes between sunrise and sunset and divide by twelve. An example is if the Sun rises at 6.27 a.m. and sets at 5.49 p.m., the amount of time contained in this day is eleven hours and twenty-two minutes. Convert this total into minutes (682) and then divide that figure by twelve (57). Therefore, each of the twelve daylight time units will be 57 minutes on that day.

Although this wonderful method of using astrology is very ancient, it may be completely new to you. You are in for a pleasant surprise though, because if you are willing to delve into a little research and put the system to the test, rich rewards are in store for you!

YOUR LUCKY DAY ★ SUNDAY

Planet ★ The Sun
Basic Energy ★ Will
Basic Magic ★ Success
Element ★ Fire
Colours ★ Yellow or Gold
Energy Keywords ★ Power, Authority, Individuality, Courage, Leadership, Determination, Faith, Dignity, Willpower, Self, Optimism, Confidence, Self-reliance, Aggression, Egocentrism, Fortitude, Loyalty, Poise, Vitality

Sunday is the day of the Sun, your ruler. In commonly used calendars, Sunday first day of the week, though in others it is the seventh. Sunday is the day of rest in most Western countries, and part of the 'weekend'. For most Christians Sunday is observed as a day of worship and rest, held as the Lord's Day, the day of Christ's resurrection. Indeed, the Russian day for Sunday is *Voskresenie*, meaning 'Resurrection day'; the Greek word for Sunday is *Kyriake*, 'the Lord's day'; and many Eastern European words for Sunday can be translated as 'without acts (no work)' *. Bloody Sunday, Easter Sunday and Palm Sunday, are three well-known days with which the Sun's day is associated.

Sunday is the day for Solar magic which helps the advancement of the individual self. It is a time when you can work towards personal healing or for a new impulse to assist your life. Sunday is commonly regarded as the best day to attract and increase overall success in all endeavours and every area of life. The ancient idea of the Sabbath (coming from a Jewish word *Shabbat*, which means 'the seventh') asks us to use this as a day of rest, rejuvenation and relaxation. You can create your own Sabbath experience any way you wish.

In the folk rhyme 'Monday's Child', 'The child that is born on the Sabbath day, is bonny and blythe and good and gay.' It is a day of Vitality, Energy, Pleasure, Optimism, Fun, Leisure, Children, Entertainment, Pure Joy and All-round Success. Yellow is the colour of the Sun, and so yellow-coloured objects such as yellow crystals and candles can be used as a magical correspondence to the Sun in spells and rituals.

* The Christian Church marks Sunday as the day of rest. However, in ancient faiths, Sunday was the day on which to celebrate the gods of the Sun, such as the Greek gods Apollo and Helios.

THE SUN'S MAGIC TIME UNITS
(BASED ON THE PLANETARY HOURS)
FOR EACH DAY OF THE WEEK

SATURDAY ★ Fourth and Eleventh time units after sunrise
SUNDAY ★ First and Eighth time units after sunrise
MONDAY ★ Fifth and Twelfth time units after sunrise
TUESDAY ★ Second and Ninth time units after sunrise
WEDNESDAY ★ Sixth time unit after sunrise
THURSDAY ★ Third and Tenth time units after sunrise
FRIDAY ★ Seventh time unit after sunrise **

Choose the Hour/s of the Sun for any transaction, exchange, initiative, activity or venture which involves wealth, willpower, success, increase, gain, prosperity, drama, pampering, joy, divination, personal power, authority, the dissolution of painful or hostile emotions and reactions, pure friendship, magic, love, compassion, bliss, determination, focus and the expansion of your gifts and talents.

** Please note that for the purposes of simplification, the information regarding 'The Sun's Magic Time Units' is a very diluted and simplified version of using magical times to your advantage. These hours cover only daylight hours, or the first twelve hours after sunrise, and do not take into account magical times after sunset or throughout the night. 'Hours' is also a deceptive term, as most 'time periods' used in this system are less than an hour, but for the purposes of simplifying the technique, I refer to them as Magic Hours (to keep with the tradition of the term 'planetary hours') rather than magic 'time units', which is what they really are. Should you wish to do further research on your ruling planet's most powerful time units, or require further information about the planet/s from which you are seeking 'energy' from in order to assist your wish-making, other sources may provide you with more comprehensive and detailed information.

A LITTLE NEW MOON / MAGICAL TIME UNIT WISH RITUAL

Step 1 ~ Choose the Magical Hour and/or day that matches your intentions. The first dawn hour of Sunday, ruled by the Sun, is a great time for all-purpose magic, success, joy, abundance, prosperity, bliss, personal power & all-round expansion.

Step 2 ~ Write out a little wish list with the appropriate coloured pen on the colour paper which corresponds to your desire.

Step 3 ~ Choose a small stone or stones of your choosing that is connected to your wish.

Step 4 ~ Find a nice patch of soil in your garden or any special place to you, dig into it, affirm your wish in your mind, place the crystal/s and piece of paper in the hole, then place a plant on top of the crystal/s and wish list.

Step 5 ~ Fill the soil back in over the roots of the plant and feed it with a little water out of a magical vessel (a small genie bottle would be ideal).

Step 6 ~ Thank the Earth, the Universe and the Sun (or whatever planet you are summoning the power from) for bringing forth your desires.

Step 7 ~ Repeat all day long: "Thank You, Thank You, Thank You!"

Step 8 ~ Watch your plant - and your wish - grow bigger and bigger as time goes on!

YOUR LUCKY CHARM/TALISMANS

The following are three 'materials' or talismanic symbols from which to make your lucky charms, and the planetary energy under which to do it, corresponding with your Sun sign:

LEO ★ Sardonyx, Heart, Gold, Sun

"When any star ascends fortunately, take a stone and herb that are under that star, make a ring of the metal that is congruous therewith, and in that fix the stone with the herb under it."
Henry Cornelius Agrippa, *On Occult Philosophy*

Charms, talismans and amulets are among the oldest forms of magic. A charm or talisman is a symbol, often used to communicate a thought, prayer or wish to, or to make a connection with the Divine. It is usually in the form of an object, which has been imbued with mysterious and magical powers. A charm may be as simple as a stone, a flower or a feather, or it might be a parchment bearing writing; the meaning and significance that you attribute to the symbol is what is important. It can be created by yourself (to best effect) or by someone else, and works as a tool to activate our subconscious mind.

You can use general charms such as a cross, or a universally lucky symbol such as a horseshoe, but you will exude and therefore attract more potency and protection if you make and wear the appropriate charms with the matching gemstone, set in the right metal and created under the corresponding planetary influence. While most people wear silver or gold, cheaper tin or copper may be more appropriate and indeed beneficial for your Sun sign. An amulet (for protection) or a talisman or charm (for luck), must also be made, ordered, designed or purchased on the appropriate day of the week for its power to be most effective. Your day, as previously described, is Sunday.

You can even go further and create or buy your amulet or charm at one of the hours and/or days when your planet is exerting its most powerful influence. It may sound complicated and requiring of forethought and effort, but if you are going to summon magic and are superstitious enough to truly *believe* that you can do this (and remember pure belief in something is the starting point of all manifestation), you should be scrupulous enough to do it properly. For your planet's day and time, please consult the information under the previous headings 'Your Lucky Day' and 'The Sun's Magic Time Units'.

GODS, GODDESSES, ANIMAL TOTEMS & OTHER 'GUIDES'

Gods, goddesses and guides can be summoned to help you live your life to its optimal best. Some are connected with your Sun sign, while others may be of your own personal choosing, ones you may feel particularly drawn towards. Those which align with your ruling planet and your Sun sign, give a good indication of those who will shine a guiding light along your desired path, but you can choose your own too, based upon exploration, observations, research, meditation or simple intuition - I believe choosing your own, based on your inner *knowing* or guidance system, is a very powerful magical tool. However, to get you started, following are some animal spirit guide ideas for your contemplation. Good luck!

YOUR LUCKY ANIMALS & BIRDS

Lion, Wolf, Hawk, Domestic Cats, Lynx, Glow-Worm, Horse, Griffin, Peacock, Swan, Rooster, Eagle, Salmon

★

"Somewhere beyond the walls of our awareness … the wilderness side, the hunter side, the seeking side of ourselves is waiting to return."
Laurens van der Post, *The Heart of the Hunter*

"(People) everywhere are being made acutely aware of the fact that something essentially to life and wellbeing is flickering very low in the human species and threatening to go out entirely. This 'something' has to do with such values as love, unselfishness, sincerity, loyalty to one's best friend, honesty, enthusiasm, humility, goodness, happiness … fun. Practically every animal has these assets in abundance and is eager to share them, given the opportunity and the encouragement."
Jay Allen Boone, *Kinship with All Life*

Some astrological systems, such as Shamanistic * or Native American Astrology, tell us that the Sun sign we were born under has a corresponding animal totem, which informs us about our characteristics and act as a kind of spiritual guide or mentor throughout our life's journey. These totems are described as Solar totems, because many of them share similarities with the Solar system and the sign the Sun was passing through at the time of our birth, and therefore relate to animals and animal behaviours which also correspond to environmental conditions and seasonal changes. These animals encompass many aspects of the Solar system, from seasonal relationships, to creature instincts, to reciprocal links with the planetary vibrations, and 'clans' within nature that you are inherently closely connected with through your date of birth.

Carl Jung, a master of dream analysis and interpretation, proposed that animals symbolise our natural instincts, operating through our dreams. He theorised that certain dream symbols, among them animals, represent core emotions and concepts, archetypes that will hold true for all of us the world over, regardless of so-called 'divisions' such as sex, customs, age or culture. In *Man and His Symbols*, Jung states that primitive societies believed that each person had a bush soul and a human soul. The bush soul incarnates as a tree or animal - a totem - and when the bush soul is harmed or injured, the human soul is considered injured as well.

Some of the most important and powerful spirit guides are those belonging to the animal kingdom. Both in ancient times and in some traditional modern tribal systems, people consult with animals for their wisdom and personal power. Even though most societies today have drifted away from this connection, it has never really left us, and different creatures continue to communicate with us on both the physical and spiritual planes in an attempt to speak to our souls and spirits.

As part of the teaching world, animals can bring us wisdom and survival skills, while others show us how to adapt, transcend or morph. Others still can remind us the importance of play and humour, and guide us around how to overcome life's challenges. Many are known for their loyalty and ability to love unconditionally and without judgement, while some have a grounded and healthy detachment, remaining true to themselves rather than pleasing others, an important lesson in itself. Whatever the qualities of the unique animal guides for your Sun sign, all have some enlightening soul-awakening traits that can teach us much about our own true inner selves. Ultimately, your animal spirit guides, and in particular your Solar totem animal, endow you with qualities that will enhance your life and help to activate your creativity, wisdom and intuition, helping to heal the broken or return the lost pieces of your soul and reconnect you to the natural world.

Your Solar totem animal (listed last on your lucky birds and animals list) is not the same as an animal spirit guide, which is based on metaphysical principles and is also based on your soul's mission in this embodiment - however, you can definitely make your birth Solar totem animal your spiritual guide if you wish, as you may find that its qualities, traits, symbolism and messages strongly reflect and define your own nature - or what you aspire to become, manifest or draw towards you. Your birth totem power animal comes from a place of trust and innocence, and represents the essence of your creative inner child. If you spend some time meditating on your Solar totem animal, asking what lessons it can teach, and reflect deeply on its character, life and habits, you may find it connects with you on a deep spiritual level and you can make the necessary changes to your life to draw in more magic and power.

Overall, if your life is stagnant or in need of healing or an energy boost, you can request your animal spirit or spirits to come and help you change your vibration, awaken your truth and arouse your inner forces. If you are aware of your animal spirit's presence in your life every day, you can use its particular energies to support, guide and teach you. And above all, pay attention to any signs and expressions of its lessons, and remember to thank your chosen animal guide for helping you.

* Shamanism is a traditional spiritual practice of the Native American culture. A shaman, one who practices this age-old art, is an intermediary between the human world and the world of the spirits. He inherits his magical powers at birth, but spends many years as an apprentice, so that he is usually much older in age before he is able to practice and call upon his skills. People ask for a shaman's help when there is a crisis on either a personal or wider spread scale, such as famine, drought, war or illness. The shaman makes contact with the spirits by going into a trance. First, he may perform a series of rituals, which usually include drumming, singing and chanting, and when these have brought on the right conditions, he leaves his body behind to travel to the other world. There he meets with the spirits of his ancestors, who inform him what must be done to relieve the suffering of his people. If the shaman is asked to cure someone of a dis-ease, then the spirits may accompany him to find the correct medicinal herbs or treatments for his patient.

YOUR FEATURE ANIMAL ★ SALMON

The Salmon's Message ★ Inspiration and motivation through example and influence
Brings the totem gift of ★ Focus, intuition, energy, activity, wisdom
Shares the power energies of ★ Motivation, purpose, noble crusades
Brings forth and teaches the magic of ★ Generosity, inspiration and confidence

Just as the lion is the king of the jungle, the Salmon is the king of the fish. It is the keeper of long life and a fruitful old age, representing power and endurance. It also teaches us to count our blessings, avoid waste, and to conserve and share. Wholly creative, electric, focused and intuitive, the Salmon's energy is palpable. A motivated leader and naturally confident, the Salmon's enthusiasm is infectious and inspiring. Generous and intelligent, the Salmon has no shortage of friends, and often has many personal crusades, on which it will be joined by others influenced by its natural charm and ability to get people onside with its ideas. Stable, calm, sensual and giving, the Salmon can also be egotistical and intolerant, but will always have a central purpose and high aims.

The word somersault conjures up images of children being nimble and playful, which is another lesson the Salmon teaches. The word somersault itself stems from the word salmon - *sault* - and was actually inspired by Salmons leaping out of the water as they made their important trip up raging rivers. Tapping into our childlike qualities is therefore another lesson we can learn from this wondrous fish.

The Salmon is also a symbol of wisdom, its wisdom including the value of returning home to regenerate, and swimming upstream through turbulent waters to gain insight and Divine messages. Its aim is to overcome all obstacles that stand in its way, and to become united with All That Is. In Celtic tales and legends, the Salmon was considered the wisest and oldest of animals, dwelling in a sacred well which was the source of the River Boyne that flowed past ancient Druid temples. These salmon would feed on hazelnuts, a reputed source of wisdom. Comparing this robust fish's journey to our own life journey can help us gain understanding as to why the Salmon was regarded as such a wise animal. It may appear that the Salmon's up-river journey to the spawning grounds is quite literally a struggle and an 'uphill battle', similar to a human's life journey. However, the reality is very different. Difficulties *are* present, but when travelling upstream, the Salmon in fact is not fighting the current, rather it travels with the reverse current that is flowing beneath the surface.

With Salmon as your power animal, significant life changes or events usually occur for you every five to seven years; the Salmon takes its long upstream journey every five to seven years, to return to the place where it was spawned, in order to spawn new life. Salmons' acute sense of smell assists them to find their way back 'home', and having unbreakable bonds with their pasts, they can remind us to honour our own heritage and origins.

In general people with this animal as their guide are tough and can persevere when others are being pulled under. Often you will choose a life that is fraught with obstacles, danger or challenges, knowing full well that within each challenge, there is a positive seed, a new beginning or an opportunity.

Another metaphor which the Salmon can help us understand, is that of their ability to overcome seemingly insurmountable obstacles and hardships to reach their goal: extremely determined, they can even jump high waterfalls to get to their destination. They struggle past numerous predators, including bears, birds of prey and humans, to reach their home waters. They have such a drive to get to their place of origin, they hardly eat and ignore almost everything else in their quest. Once they finally arrive, they simply spawn and die. Through this amazing life cycle, the Salmon can teach us that no matter where we are, we are always on our way 'home', that place of sacred beginnings that resides within us all, and that we must seek an understanding of our history, through frequently going back to our childhoods in our minds to achieve that understanding and *knowing*.

Salmon medicine helps us to flow with the currents beneath the surface. We must be determined, but also open to the simple flow of life, which will carry us along and support us if we allow it to. After all, the Salmon can teach you the wisdom that being light-hearted, joyful, open and innocent is not the aid to reaching the goal, but the goal itself. Somersaults, of course, are optional.

SPIRITUAL KEEPER ★ COYOTE

Your spiritual keeper guides your spiritual growth and brings illumination. Your spiritual keeper is determined by the season in which you were born. Regarded as the 'keepers' or 'caretakers' of the Universe, the four Directions or alignments were also referred to by the Native Americans as the Four Winds because their presence was *felt* rather than seen. The Direction to which your birth time belongs influences the nature of your inner senses. The South Direction's totem is the Coyote. The Coyote is a symbol of growth, fruition, emotions, productivity and fluidity. The Coyote is bold, impetuous, charming, youthful and creative, and as a spiritual keeper, can endow us with these qualities. In some native tribes, the Coyote is referred to as a trickster or joker. A clever, cunning and amazingly adaptable animal, its message is of wisdom and folly. Operating year-round, the Coyote doesn't try to trick us, but rather mirrors our own human capacity for stupidity and cleverness.

Challenging the status quo, the Coyote sometimes becomes unstuck but is ever the triumphant survivor. To the Indian, this animal is a creator, teacher and keeper of magic, and even when the magic does not work, it serves a purpose; the Coyote knows there is always hidden wisdom. Playful as well as skilful and agile, the Coyote teaches us not to take things too seriously, and that anything is possible if we understand that wisdom, balance, intellect and fun can all co-exist. Through this spiritual keeper, we can reawaken the child within, stimulate our intuition and open up the mind. Coyotes hunt in cooperative groups, in an organised fashion - while one chases, one will rest, then they switch - which can teach the value of teamwork. The howl of this animal is a social call, usually warning of danger or to bring attention to its loneliness, reminding us too of our own primal needs and connections.

The Coyote's teachings can help you negotiate a difficult situation, and can highlight the traps we may be caught in, or ways we could be fooling ourselves. It is an especially powerful healer when it comes to relationships, because it is when we are in one that we often fool ourselves the most. Following the Coyote won't make you a fortune, but its lesson is to teach us that material wealth doesn't equate to true happiness anyway. Your animal keeper the Coyote is, above all, a potent symbol of the need for the balance between wisdom, trickery, skill, cleverness and cunning.

CLAN ★ THUNDERBIRD (OR HAWK)

Your clan animal comes from a place of inner knowing and intuition, helping you to discover the essence and magic of your true self. The Thunderbird, sometimes referred to as Hawk, is a Totem of the Fire clan, and its medicine is messenger. Thunderbird holds the Fire clan and brings thunder, lightning and rain. The greatest of all the winged creatures, the Thunderbird is closest to the Creator.

His Fire and spark carry the gift of life and link the soul to the Great Mystery. Thunderbird people are doers, often leaders, and are usually found in the spotlight expressing their feelings. Naturally invigorated by thunder and lightning, Thunderbird clan people are energised by the air just before and after a storm. Ever seeking a higher union with Spirit, Thunderbird souls have a responsibility to all the aspects of their element - Fire, Sun and lightning - and it is important for them to understand the power and purpose of these things. As trailblazers of the other three clans, they are born with the drive to initiate and to function within the greater tribe of Humanity, progressing it by broadening boundaries. You are not travelling the Great Road to build or to harvest, but rather you are forging the way ahead in preparation for the planting and harvesting that will be done by the other clans. The challenge for the Thunderbird clan is to learn the virtues of patience, for to effectively utilise our natural gifts we must also be aware of our polar opposites - and integrate the two to create a meaningful input that yields fulfilment and results for the benefit of ourselves and others.

Visualise the Thunderbird/Hawk in your spirit to be soaring high and being held aloft by the invisible hands of the Four Winds. Your eyes scan all before you and above you, and your keen perception is without equal. The Thunderbird's true desire is not to know what lies below; your true yearning is to join with Grandfather Sky. Fly high and keep your eyes focused ever upward.

THE GRIFFIN & LEO

The griffin is a mythological creature common in the Middle East. It has the head and wings of an eagle, the body of a lion and sometimes a serpent's tail. Because it has the head of an eagle and the body of a lion it is said to represent both land and air. Considered Divinely powerful and majestic, it is a Solar symbol and as such it symbolises the power of the Sun - and of Leo. Altogether the griffin is a very powerful symbol, whose roles have been, among many, of treasure protection and gold guardianship. To many cultures, it is regarded as the King of birds and Lord of the Air.

YOUR CORRESPONDING CHINESE ASTROLOGY ANIMAL

The Chinese Zodiac, known as Sheng Xiao (literally meaning 'birth likeness'), is based on a twelve-year cycle, each year in that cycle related to a particular animal. These animals are: Rat, Ox, Tiger, Rabbit, Dragon, Snake, Horse, Sheep, Monkey, Rooster, Dog and Pig. The selection and order of the animals that so influence people's lives, particularly in East Asian cultures, originated in the Han Dynasty (202 BC - 220 AD) and was based upon each animal's traits, characteristics, tendencies and living habits. Further, ancient people observed that there were twelve Full Moons in a year, and that, among other similarly related celestial observations, suggests its origins are also based on astronomical concepts.

The legend of the Chinese zodiac's story usually begins with the Jade Emperor, or Buddha (depending on who is telling the tale), summoning all the animals of the Universe for a race or a banquet. The twelve animals of the zodiac all appeared at the palace, and the order in which they arrived determined the order of the Chinese zodiac.

Each oriental animal corresponds with a Western astrology sign. For Leo, it is the Monkey.

> "I am the seasoned traveller
> Of the Labyrinth.
> The genius of alacrity,
> Wizard of the impossible.
> My brilliance is yet unmatched
> In its originality.
> My heart's filled with potent magic
> That could cast a hundred spells.
> I am put together
> For mine own pleasure.
> *I am the Monkey."*
> **Theodora Lau**

Chinese name for the Monkey ★ HOU
Ranking Order ★ Ninth
Hours ruled by the Monkey ★ 3 p.m. to 5 p.m.
Direction ★ West - Southwest
Season and principle month ★ Summer - August
Corresponds to the Western sign ★ Leo

★ **MONKEY** ★ *Fixed Element Metal*

★ Keywords ★

Desire for Knowledge, Intelligent, Skilful, Inventive, Cunning, Dexterous, Curious, Daring, Easily Discouraged, Strong-willed, Vain, Mischievous, Improvising, Zealous

The Monkey is the ninth sign of the Chinese horoscope. Traditionally a yang sign, the Monkey's characteristics are inventiveness, vigour and wit. Adept at problem-solving, Monkeys are humorous and resourceful. Like the creature itself, you are a clever trickster with an extroverted, outgoing and technically adept nature. Known for your humour and mischief, you can also be very conscientious as well as skilled, so you take pride in doing any job very well. A great problem-solver, your mental dexterity comes to the fore under pressure and you will use unusual methods to solve problems that leave others stumped. On top of this, you are an excellent communicator, but may become deceitful and opportunistic when it suits your purpose.

YOUR METALS

Leonine power metals are Gold, Platinum, Copper and Bronze.

Although the magic power of crystals is widely recognised and applied, the influence radiating from metals is often overlooked. Metal, too, emits a powerful energy and in fact, in Chinese philosophy, metal is considered so essential and powerful that it is classified as one of the elements, alongside Air, Fire, Earth and Water.

As already mentioned earlier in the book, throughout the writings of early philosophers and theorists, there are countless references to the unmistakable mystic connection between the seven known planets of the time, and Earthly affairs, ailments and objects. Seven metals were connected with the seven planets, to which seven colours and the seven 'transformations' were added. So the ancient alchemist came to share the astrological doctrine that each planet ruled a mineral: The Sun ruled gold, the Moon silver, Mars iron, Venus copper, Saturn lead, Jupiter tin, and Mercury quicksilver. Consequently, in alchemical symbolism the same sign came to represent the nominated metal and its corresponding planet.

GOLD

"Gold stands for truth, consciousness and eternity ...
the Cosmic impulse descends from the highest,

Divine level to the material earthly world, taking on form and substance as it does so. This is absolutely within the nature of things. In alchemical terms, this means that the eternal essence of gold came into creation and took on denser and darker forms as it became manifest, until only the seed of gold remained buried in the primal material."

C. Gilchrist, *Everyday Alchemy*

Gold is a chemical element with symbol Au (from Latin *aurum*, meaning 'gold', but has its roots in Proto-Germanic meaning 'shine'), and in its purest form it is a malleable, ductile, soft, dense, bright, slightly reddish-yellow metal. It has been a valuable and highly-sought after precious metal used for coinage, jewellery, and other arts since long before the beginning of recorded history.

Known and valued since ancient times, gold is most commonly associated with jewellery and currency but symbolically its most powerful association is with the Sun, ruler of Leo. It also has a connection with hermetic alchemy. It stands for purity, wisdom, Earthly power and glory, spiritual enlightenment, nobility and of course, wealth. Gold is associated with deities either physically or as a representation. The Incas sprayed their rulers with gold dust, literally turning them into a 'gold man', and the ancient Egyptians believed that the flesh of their Sun god Ra was made of gold. Other cultures believed, and many still believe, that gold was the Earthly manifestation of their gods or of the Sun itself.

Gold reflects the Sun's (perceived) colour and brilliance. It is thought to be incorruptible and incapable of corrosion. With long-held beliefs around and links to wealth, medieval alchemists sought the 'philosophic gold', not necessarily to attain literal riches, but for its gift of eternal life.

Precious metals often occur in their pure, natural state, turning up in veins - mineral deposits that fill the cracks in Earth's crust. They can also be found mixed with sand and gravel on riverbeds. These deposits form when erosion separates the metal from rock and water washes it into a river, where it sinks to the bottom - as often happens with gold.

Gold is used widely in jewellery, but it has properties which make it valuable in other industries too. For example, gold does not rust, so it is often used to make vital pieces of electronic equipment. It is also very shiny and radiant, so when used as a coating on the outside of satellites and other space instruments, gold reflects cosmic radiation that would otherwise damage the equipment. The global consumption of new gold produced is about 50 per cent in jewellery, 40 per cent in investments, and 10 per cent in industry.

Great human achievements are frequently rewarded with gold medals, golden trophies and other such symbols. Similarly, gold is associated with perfect or Divine principles, such as the 'golden rule' and the 'golden egg'. Our most valued older years are often considered our 'golden years', and the height of a civilisation is referred to as its 'golden age'. Overall, it is a cultural symbol of wealth, abundance, enlightenment and success.

It's not all bright news however. Gold production is associated with contributing to hazardous pollution, and cyanide spills and mercury compounds reaching waterways, causing heavy metal contamination, are considered dangerous both to the environment and to the health of living organisms. When the used ore is dumped as waste, these dumps create long-term, highly hazardous wastes second only to nuclear waste dumps. Gold extraction is also a highly energy-intensive industry, using an enormous amount of electricity in the extraction and grinding processes.

Pure metallic (elemental) gold is non-toxic and non-irritating when ingested, and is sometimes used as a food decoration in the form of gold leaf. Metallic gold is a component of some alcoholic drinks, and is approved as a food additive in the EU. Now step up to receive your gold medal and say cheers to a glass of Gold Strike!

Note ★ As gold is expensive, bronze or brass are often used as substitutes. Brass is primarily used when the main purpose of a charm is for protection or to attract money. Pyrite, or fool's gold, is often used for prosperity charms. Gold combines well with amber for a success amulet. Gold charms are used for promoting wisdom, increasing courage and confidence, and success in general.

PLATINUM

The word 'platinum' originates from the Spanish word *plata*, meaning 'silver', referring to the colour of the metal. Platinum was discovered in the early 1700s. It is so rare that two million pounds of ore may only contain about one pound of platinum metal. Its rarity makes it even more valuable than gold. Platinum nuggets are rarely larger than a pea - anything larger would qualify as a major find. The highest quality platinum comes from the Ural Mountains in Russia. It can be used for jewellery, but has less glamorous uses too: it is placed in anti-pollution devices in cars to trap dirt and toxic gases.

PLANTS, HERBS, SPICES, TREES, SHRUBS, FLOWERS, SCENTS & INCENSE

Plants have long been associated with magic, medicinal properties, superstition, nutrition and even astrology. In ancient times, some were endowed with magical properties based upon beliefs of the time, but also upon anecdotal evidence that some herbal concoctions, flowers or essences helped alleviate and even cure uncomfortable, painful or dis-eased physical or mental states. Whether these were based upon 'old wives' tales' or beliefs in supernatural forces matters little, for in modern times we can prove and indeed *have* proven through scientific research and controlled experiments, that plants have their place in our health and medicine cabinets. Some 'magical' plants have aphrodisiac or narcotic properties, while others have formidable toxic effects, but all are considered in some way to affect the human system on physical, spiritual and psychological levels. Plants such as cocoa, tobacco and coffee, which have accompanied humans over the course of millennia, are still, more than ever, an integral part of our daily lives. They still incite the same pleasures, the same fascinations, and the same dangers, and some still carry the same taboos. It is interesting to note that more than 80 per cent of chemical medicines in existence today, and found in pharmacists' dispensaries, are made from plants.

In modern astrology herbs are often associated with the zodiac signs and have evolved from an old system where a specific planet rules each herb. The planet that governs a herb is chosen according to its appearance, scent and where it grows; herbs are additionally categorised as hot or cold, and dry or moist. In this way you can see how the nature of the herb corresponds to the nature of the planet. If you are familiar with your ruling planets' basic associations, you will find it easy to match it to herbs. Although you can simply buy whatever herbs you wish to use for your magic, the optimum effect will be obtained if you can gather them at a favourable astrological time. Once you are armed with astrological knowledge, you can choose a time when the planet that rules your chosen herb is in a position of strength. Keep in mind that each planet rules a substantial amount of plants, so if one isn't easily obtained, it should be simply to find another one to use for the same purpose.

There sometimes seems to be a wide variance in the list of herbs associated with a specific astrological influence. This is because the different parts of the plant have different rulerships and uses. For example, whichever planet rules it, a plant that bears fruit is naturally related to Jupiter, its flowers relate to Venus, seed or bark to Mercury, leaves to the Moon, wood to Mars, and roots to Saturn. So, as well as the planet that traditionally rules the plant, it can be regarded as having a secondary ruler according to the part of the plant being used. Although you don't need to work with a highly complex system of deciding which herb will suit your purposes, you can make your magical workings more powerful by paying attention to some of these nuances.

Essentially, different scents, herbs, flowers and plants have their own specific vibrations. Their essences should be worn on your skin (you can make up your own combinations using essential oils or flower waters), burned in an oil burner, inhaled from a cloth, diffused in a bath or bowl of steam, or burned as incense sticks. Many plants, herbs and spices, however used, contain gentle yet effective energies which will affect not only your wishing ceremonies, but also your moods, associations and emotions, which can assist in carrying your wonderful Self in the direction of your dreams. Lifted up on incense smoke, for example, your wish is carried out to the wider Universe. Try making your own, out of any or all of your power plants, woods, flowers, shrubs, trees or herbs!

Thirty-three magical, mythical plants are: Cocoa, rosemary, tobacco, thyme, wheat, coffee, sugar cane, cinnamon, hemp, tea, pumpkin, foxglove, incense, amanita (a mushroom), tarragon, pepper, rice, belladonna, reed, ginseng, clove, ginger, sage, maize, mistletoe, lily, mandrake, St John's Wort, poppy, peyote, cinchona, verbena and the vine *. How many of your Leonine 'lucky plants' (listed under the next sub-category, 'Your Lucky Plants, Herbs, Spices', etc.) can be found on this Magical 33 List?

YOUR LUCKY PLANTS, HERBS, SPICES, TREES, SHRUBS, FLOWERS, SCENTS, OILS & INCENSE

Olive, Saffron, Liquorice, Sunflower, Dandelion, Turmeric, Cinnamon, Aniseed, Mustard, Ginger,

Sage, Palm, Sunflower Seeds, Fennel, Chamomile, Lotus **, Nutmeg, Rosemary, Bay Leaves, Borage, Marigold, Peony, Citrus Trees, Juniper, Wake Robin, Dill, Walnut, Cedar, Bay Laurel, Eyebright, Daffodil, Mistletoe, Passionflower, Yellow Lily, Motherwort, Cowslip, St John's Wort, Heliotrope *.

For the Sun ★ Rosemary, St John's Wort, Saffron, Chamomile, Oak. The Sun takes a year to pass through all twelve signs of the zodiac. Consequently, the plants associated with it are usually annuals, such as Calendula, Sunflower, Sassafras & Cinnamon *

* Some plant products can be poisonous, toxic, hallucinogenic or even fatal if consumed. Always research first.

** A Note on the Lotus Flower ★ The lotus flower - which has its roots in the mud but arises out of it beautiful and clean - is a symbol of how we can all rise, glorious and triumphant, from the muddiest of conditions. Indeed, Hindus and Buddhists consider the lotus an emblem of purity, as its beautiful flower comes from a plant that grows in slime. The Ancient Egyptians believed the goddess Isis was born from a lotus flower, and so they associated the lotus with fertility and sexual potency. The Hindus believe the creator god Brahma was born from a golden lotus flower that was cited in the navel of the Universe. And one legend about Buddha tells that everywhere he walked, he left lotuses behind him instead of footprints. The lotus holds a spiritual significance and meaning for many traditions. Across all, the lotus is a symbol of creation: out of the mud, the world can be born. It is also a symbol of wisdom, expressing the truth about the possibilities for all living things. The Buddhist mantra

"Om mani Padme hum" translates as "Om, jewel in the lotus, amen." Reciting this mantra is said to bring peace to the chanter and to those nearby. A thousand-petalled lotus symbolises spiritual enlightenment.

YOUR SPECIAL POWER FLOWERS

LEO IN GENERAL ★ Sunflower ★ The sunflower, brought to Europe from the Americas, was called *girasol* by Spanish explorers, which means "turn to the Sun." It was sacred to the Incas who used it extensively in carvings and jewellery. Because the sunflower turns toward the Sun, it became associated with devotion to God. In China, the sunflower symbolised immortality, and people ate sunflower seeds in the hope of living long and happy lives.

OTHER BIRTH FLOWERS ★ Cowslip, Forsythia, Passionflower, Peony & Heliotrope

JULY BORN ★ Larkspur or Delphinium ★ Named for the irrepressible dolphin (from the Greek delphis), the blooming delphinium bestows health and a talent for happiness upon those born in July.

AUGUST BORN ★ Poppy ★ Opium, used to relieve pain and induce sleep, was originally made from a variety of poppy commonly found around the Mediterranean, before its cultivation spread along the Silk Road through Asia and finally China, where it became the catalyst for the Opium Wars of the mid-1800s. The Greeks associated it with Hypnos, the god of sleep, and Morpheus, the god of dreams (morphine is made from opium and was named after Morpheus). In Greek mythology, Persephone was picking poppies when Hades abducted her. Since World War I, the poppy has been adopted as the flower of remembrance in the British Commonwealth, and millions of artificial poppy flowers are sold each year to be worn on Remembrance Day. Because it produces a large amount of seeds, the poppy is associated with fertility. The poppy's many blessings are a capacity for renewal, and an understanding that there's a time for every purpose: beauty, loss, loyalty and courage.

YOUR FOODS

Serve them as royalty or don't serve them at all. Resplendent, adventurous and theatrical, the roaring big cat is just a Leo waiting for his banquet dinner! Flamboyant, dramatic, larger-than-life and jolly, the Lion loves being waited on and pampered by others - especially with lashings of food. Your ruling planet the Sun rules the colours red, orange and yellow, and is associated with heat and fire, therefore hot and spicy foods probably appeal. Leonines are extravagant in most areas of life, culinary delights included. The more condiments and garnishes and fancy add-ons, the better. You are definitely an advocate for, "You eat with your eyes first," because you adore fine presentation. Being a Lion, you enjoy hearty, dense, warming cuisine, and would always opt for a hot roast dinner over a cold salad. Adventurous, bold and all-embracing, you are likely to enjoy a vast variety of foods, and because of your proneness to try anything, you often over-indulge and suffer for it. Rich, exotic, luxurious and refined foods appeal to you, such as caviar, oysters, cheeses, desserts, chocolate (you are the most likely sign to be a chocoholic), hors douvres, and pretty much anything gourmet or fancy; in fact, the more expensive and well-presented the dish, the more appealing you will find it! Anything gold-dusted scores an honourable mention in your recipe book too. Bland, messy, tedious, sloppy, insubstantial, colourless, boring and poorly presented are definitely not on the menu for the Lion.

LEO POWER FOODS

"Let food be your medicine; let medicine be your food."
Hippocrates

Walnuts, Meat, Eggs, Parsley, Spinach, Kale, Watercress, Honey, Rich, Spicy, Hot and Dry, Aromatic, Sweet and Sour Foods. Yellow and Orange-coloured Citrus Fruits (Oranges, Lemons, Grapefruit, Tangerines), Mangoes, Nectarines, Orange Vegetables (Sweet Potato, Pumpkin, Yams, Carrot), the Flesh of the Heart, Sunflower Oil and Margarine, Curries, Rice, Cabbage and Eggplant also appeal to the Leonine palate. Your power beverages are Cider, Lemon Squash, Tea, Luxury Liqueurs, Cocktails, and Fortified and Expensive Wines. *

* Caution: Always use essential oils, alcohol and/or herbs with caution and research each one prior to use, as not all are safe for use by certain people, or under certain conditions such as pregnancy, intoxication or illness. Some herbs and oils may be hallucinogenic, toxic in high doses, or produce other undesirable effects, and may be considered potentially harmful or hazardous if used or consumed before operating machinery, driving, or combined with alcohol or other drugs. Always consult a qualified practitioner or undertake thorough research from reliable sources before use or consumption of any of the listed essential oils, herbs or foods.

YOUR LUCKY WOOD ★ WALNUT
(Great to make a magic wand out of!)

Native Americans referred to trees as 'Standing People' because they stand firm, obtaining strength from their connection with the Earth. They therefore teach us the importance of being grounded, while at the same time listening to, and reaching towards, our higher aspirations. In Norse mythology, Yggdrasil, the tree of life, is a cosmic map that represents all life. The tree has its roots in the Underworld, is linked to the Earth through its trunk and its branches reach into the air of the Otherworld of spirit. The dryad, or tree's spirit, needs to be respected and asked when 'taking' from a tree for the purposes of magic. The essence of tree magic lies in understanding the qualities of each type. These can be drawn on for such things as healing and spell-casting. For example, the rowan tree grows high up the sides of mountains, often in hard-to-reach places, so if you need to develop tenacity or access to difficult spiritual spaces, you can call on this tree; the oak tree is durable and strong, so if you are needing fortification or firmness, you can gain power from this tree. When respected as living, breathing beings, trees can provide insights into the workings of Nature, cycles, and our own inner essence. Each birth time is associated with a particular kind of tree, the basic qualities of which complement the nature of those born during that time. Appreciate the beauty of your affinity tree and study its nature carefully, for it has a connection with your own nature and lessons to impart.

WALNUT ★ Walnut wood teaches us clarity and focus, and how to use our intelligence and other mind gifts wisely. Holding the powers of teleportation, inspiration, the breath and astral travel, walnut is symbolic of mental wisdom.

YOUR SACRED CELTIC CALENDAR TREES ★ HOLLY OR HAZEL

HOLLY ★ (8 July - 4 August)
HAZEL ★ (5 August - 1 September)

The Celts and other ancient peoples had many beliefs and traditions based around the magical lore of trees. The system of Celtic tree astrology was developed out of a natural connection with the Druids' knowledge of Earth cycles and their reverence for the sacred knowledge they believed was held by trees. The Druids had a profound connection with trees and regarded them as vessels of infinite wisdom. Their calendar, being based on a Lunar year of thirteen months, contains a tree for each of these Lunar months, corresponding with (but not exactly) each of the twelve western astrology zodiac signs, which are based on the Solar calendar. Because there are some crossovers, I have included two possible trees for your zodiacal birth period.

HOLLY ★ Holly is traditionally associated with Christmas, and is used to decorate homes at Winter Solstice. Its red berries and green leaves in the dead of (northern hemisphere) winter symbolise everlasting life. Holly carries properties of exorcism, healing and purification. With its protective qualities, a holly tree grown near the home is thought to provide protection from thunder, lightning and demons. A masculine tree, the prickly leaves of the holly match its formidable associations as a tree of protection and warfare, and its wood was used to make spears and chariot wheels in ancient times.

The holly is a sacred tree of the Sun and is associated with the Sun god in Wiccan beliefs. The roots of this belief lie in the tree's hardy, evergreen qualities and its connection to the Winter Solstice, as the shortest day of the year symbolises the rebirth of the Sun, and the Wheel of the Year now turns towards the summer. Evergreens have a special significance with the Winter Solstice: they represent the undying light of the Solar influence as they retain their leaves all year.

The fine, hard wood of this tree is especially good for carving and inlay work, and its wood, berries, leaves and flowers, can be used in many spells, magical tools and charms. Its best known use is the tradition originating from the medieval practice of hanging a 'Holy Bough' made from holly and other evergreens, in the entrance of homes at Christmas, to welcome guests. This gesture also symbolised goodwill and longevity.

Holly carries a regal status in Celtic tree astrology. High-minded and noble, those born during the holly period are said to have no issues taking on roles of leadership and power. You take on challenges with ease, overcoming them with vigilance, skill and tact, meaning you are seldom defeated. You are competitive, ambitious and confident, which may make you come across as arrogant, but under the façade you are generous, kind and affectionate. But because many things come to you so easily, you have a tendency to rest on your laurels and can become lazy and complacent.

HAZEL ★ Hazel is said to bring luck, fertility, protection, wisdom and wishes. Celebrated in Celtic folklore as a tree of knowledge, poetry and learning, the hazel tree is reputed to have 'nine hazelnuts of wisdom', which in Celtic legend, fell into a sacred pool or well and were eaten by salmon. According to the story, the fish, called Fintan, imbibed the nine hazelnuts of wisdom and each one consumed became a spot on its scales. Whoever ate the salmon would then receive infinite wisdom. Its connection with the god Thor also associates it with Fire, virility, matters of the heart and childbirth. The nuts, used as charms and love tokens, signified the hazel tree's blessing of fertility, birth and the successful raising of children.

Hazel wood is pliant and has traditionally been used for divining underground water. A hazelnut on a string also makes a good dowsing pendulum. Its flexibility also made it a valuable wood for making walking sticks, fishing rods, whip handles and baskets.

Hazel types are usually efficient, highly intelligent and organised. Naturally gifted in academia, you have an ability to recall and retain information with amazing accuracy. You're well-informed and know your facts; generally smart and with an impressive knowledge base, you like things to be ordered, structured, controlled and 'just so', which can sometimes lead to compulsive behaviours. You like rules, although you are typically making them rather than playing by them.

ESPECIALLY FOR AUSTRALIANS
(OF ALL ZODIAC SIGNS)

If you live in Australia, here are two Australian-based magical woods, for those who prefer to source their woods closer to home and nature. Australia has a less documented history than many European civilisations, but still has no less mythology and legends swirling in its mists of time.

EUCALYPTUS ★ Eucalyptus is very plentiful and has a wonderfully intoxicating, distinctive, clean aroma which is reminiscent of the continent's vast areas of bushland, and has played an important ceremonial and medicinal role in the culture of Australian Aborigines, who have inhabited the nation for 40,000 to 50,000 years. Eucalyptus is a wood of feminine energy whose elemental association is Earth and main origin is Australia. One of the strongest healing woods known, eucalyptus wood has been used for centuries for medicinal as well as ritualistic purposes. Heady and Earthy, the energy of this wood is clean and pure. Eucalyptus is recommended for the promotion of good, robust health, and is also related to luck, especially if regarding knowledge. An excellent tool in divination, particularly when worn as a charm to invoke luck, it brings the wearer or user good fortune when used in rituals seeking positive results.

LEOPARDWOOD (or LACEWOOD) ★
Leopardwood or the Leopard Tree, so named because of its spotted wood, carries the energies of both the masculine and the feminine, Mars (Aries, Scorpio) and Venus (Taurus, Libra), and its main affinity is with the Water element (Cancer, Scorpio, Pisces). Leopardwood is a very useful tool for divination and is associated with positive luck, earning it the label 'gambler's wood'. Overall, its energy is very positive, making it an ideal wood for use in almost any ritual or spell, especially those concerning luck, magic and divination.

THE POWER OF LOVE

Each Sun sign exudes their own love and romance style. This style is an energy unique to that sign, and has the power to magnetise to that person their true, soulful match. Unhappy or unsuccessful relationships are often the result of incompatible Sun signs, personal values, goals, hopes, viewpoints or expectations. I believe everyone has a perfect soul partner (or three!) who is especially for them, and just knowing that special person or persons are out there can illuminate your life's romantic path. In this lifetime, we may not find that person or persons, but can still experience the joys and wonders of many other significant relationships which enrich and add tremendous meaning to our lives. Some partnerships are only fleeting, but the feelings they give us can last a lifetime, while others are more enduring, and the rewards they give us and lessons they teach us can last a lifetime too. Small gestures of love on a frequent basis, consistent nurturing and communication, and making the effort to understand each other, are just four ways to keep the fires of passion and romance burning long after the initially roaring fire has diminished into glowing embers.

Your whole natal chart would need to be examined to form an overall picture of your romantic nature, and although the Sun is a fantastic starting point, it is not the sole consideration. Regarding these other planets, in Carl Jung's studies on psychological astrology, and in traditional synastry (the comparing of two people's natal charts to determine overall compatibility), the harmonious link between the Sun in one person's chart and the Moon in the other's (usually the man's Sun and the woman's Moon) is considered the best indication for a happy and enduring relationship. More specifically, the sextile aspect, an angle of 60 degrees, appeared most frequently between the Sun of one and the Moon of the other in fulfilling relationships. Other positive planetary contacts, such as one person's Moon to another's Venus, or the Mars to the Moon (again, traditional indications of attraction and harmony) also occurred frequently.

The feminine personal planets in a male's chart (Moon and Venus), and the masculine personal planets in a female's chart (Sun and Mars) tell a lot about the inner self and how this is projected onto relationships. However helpful chart analysis is in telling a story about your relationship style and approach, it all depends not on your chart, but on what you do with the resources at your disposal, which your chart can indeed tell you a lot about. Relationships and marriages involving harmonious planetary and zodiacal energies between the two people tend to last longer because they are simply more 'flowing' and easier.

The signs in which the four personal and 'relationship' planets - the Sun, the Moon, Venus and Mars - are placed, coupled with the aspects they make with the other planets in the chart, give important clues into understanding the often unconscious drives within you that shape your relating style, tastes, mannerisms and patterns.

Expanding upon the other planetary considerations is beyond the scope of this book, but it is useful to know, particularly if you are interested in examining the dynamics of a current relationship a bit deeper, or are wishing to attract a new one into your life. But for now, your Sun sign is a wonderful place to start! Your Solar sign is regarded as being at the core of the complex - and very fun - study of relationships! So for now, we will begin this study of love with your essence, your core self, the brightest light shining from within - your Sun sign!

SOME LUCKY-IN-LOVE TIPS
GENERAL HINTS

★ To attract and retain love, the Heart chakra (an energy centre within the body) needs to be balanced and clear from blockages. The Heart chakra is located in the region of the physical heart. Its Sanskrit name is *anahata*, and its symbol is a twelve-petal green lotus flower whose centre contains a green circle and two intersecting triangles making up a six-pointed star representing balance (and also could be said to symbolise six as the number of Venus). Its element is Air and its colour is green. Balance in this chakra is expressed as unconditional love for ourselves and others. Crystals that can be used to cleanse and balance this chakra are mostly green and pink stones.

★ Pink candles (two, representing a couple, or six, representing Venus, is preferable) can be used in love spells.

★ Any 'love-attracting' wishing rituals should be done on a Friday (ruled by Venus) night around the time of the New Moon (signifying the principle of increase and growth).

★ Basil, otherwise known as witch's herb or St Joseph's wort, is said to be the most potent lover herb of all. Basil vibrates to the energy of Mars, which is all about lust and sexual energy, and it is used prolifically in all sorts of love potions and rituals throughout the world.

★ Ginger has a reputation as a potent sexual tonic and aphrodisiac *. Arousing and warm, it can increase sensual vitality, particularly in men. Being warming and spicy, its vibration aligns with Mars. Saffron is also regarded as a potent, albeit expensive, aphrodisiac!

★ Wear red and pink (associated with Mars and Venus respectively), as these colours in all their shades are said to incite passion, lust and romance. Green is also connected with the heart by virtue of its association with the Heart chakra and the planet Venus, and its links with fertility, nature, abundance of all kinds, and new growth.

★ Call upon some higher spiritual help. When working your 'love magic', some planetary influences, goddesses and gods that you can call upon are: Aphrodite, Venus and Eros/Cupid, and other lesser known deities such as Juno Lucina, Demeter, Freya, Ishtar, Circe and Hathor.

★ The planet Venus has developed a rich culture of gods and goddesses associated with her varying levels of love and passion. These include the virgin - Brighid; the fertile woman - Aphrodite, (the Greek goddess); and of course Venus (the Roman equivalent); the mother and provider - Demeter; and desirous or physical love - Eros/Cupid (Venus's son).

★ The pine tree is sacred to Adonis (Venus's lover) and is said to balance the male and female energies. Pine is cleansing and protective and, as an evergreen, symbolises life. Its cones represent fertility.

★ Cardamom is said to have aphrodisiac qualities.

★ The three almost universally recognised symbols of love are the goddesses Venus and Aphrodite, and the Cupid. Venus is the patroness of flowers and vegetation, and represents the regenerative cycle of creation, as well as beauty, herbs and physical love. She can be called upon for general love wishes and rituals. The dove, roses, rings, copper, apples, rosemary and the ankh are some of her sacred symbols. Aphrodite is a Greek goddess who has the ability to brings lovers together. Her name means 'of the sea' as she is believed to have been born of the foam of the ocean. She can be called upon in ceremonies and spells for affection, love, marriage and partnership. Some of her associated symbols are the Flower of Aphrodite, swans, dolphins, frankincense and myrrh. Cupid, the cherubic winged boy with a bow and arrow, is the Roman name, and Eros is the Greek name for the same deity. The son of Venus/Aphrodite, he is an aspect that represents lustful love and desire.

★ Heartsease, another name for the wild pansy, Latin viola tricolour, was one of the most popular additives to the love potions of the ancient Romans and Greeks.

★ In centuries past, when people were more in tune with nature and its cycles, ceremonies, rituals and festivals were held on certain dates or times of year. The following are some examples, and you can reawaken their powers through craft and ceremony: February 2 is Bridhid's Day, or Bride's Day, and represents the white goddess; February 14 is Valentine's Day, traditionally the greatest and most well-known love 'celebration' of the year; March 1 is one of the festival days of Juno Lucina, the light bearer and goddess of women and marriage; the month of April is especially linked to the love goddess Aphrodite; the Summer solstice which falls on or around June 21 is an important time for reconnecting with the spirit of love, fertility and marriage; August 1 is the first of three harvest festivals in the Celtic calendar: The Harvest Festival honours Demeter, the goddess of love, as bountiful mother and faithful wife; the Festival of Lights, Diwali, in October, is sacred to Lakshmi, the Hindu goddess of happiness, love, and good fortune; the Winter solstice which falls on or around December 21, marks the turning point from long dark nights to lengthening days, and is the time of the wheel of love when virgin goddesses gave birth to their children - it is also fittingly symbolised by evergreens such as pine, ivy and holly; in Mexico, December 31, the last night of the year, is traditionally 'wishing night' and is an opportune time to make a wish for a lover in the coming year, using evergreen branches to enhance your request.

* The term 'aphrodisiac' is derived from Aphrodite, the Greek goddess of love, beauty, lust and sensuality

★ GEMSTONES ★

When it comes to calling love into your life using crystals, the general rule is that any of the pink or green stones are closely aligned with matters of the heart and can therefore help you to entice the affections you seek. Although your Sun sign has its very own special gemstones, outlined elsewhere in the book, the following stones can be used by all the signs (except for the first point, which are your own sign's feature stones), as their energies and qualities contain the power to attract and create love in all its forms, from self-love to deeper soulful connections with another, or to increase states of being which open the heart, thus enhancing your abilities to magnetise love.

★ Citrine, Ruby and Peridot ★ Using your Leonine luckiest crystals is a fabulous start to working on heightening your romantic zest, and making your sensual energy more potent. Onyx, Carnelian and Sardonyx are also useful in raising your attracting powers.

★ Rose Quartz is the ultimate love stone. It invites love into your life by helping to open your heart to receive love, and gently reminding you that you are worthy of love. Connected with the Heart chakra, it is the stone of unconditional love, enhancing all forms of it and opening up the heart. It is excellent for increasing self-worth and acceptance. The colour of rose quartz is pink, the colour of Venus, the amorous planet of desire and nurturance. Balancing and calming, it helps to heal emotional pain. Wear this stone, keep some beside your bed, or sleep with some under your pillow to remind you that love it coming your way - and that you whole*heart*edly deserve it!

★ Green Aventurine is considered the 'opportunity and luck stone'. Connected with the Heart chakra, it helps us to recognise opportunities and is said to place us exactly where we need to be for good things to transpire, as energetically it opens our mind and heart to increased perception to recognise lucky elements. It also promotes new growth, optimism, and is an overall attractor of good fortune, adventure and abundance.

★ Jade, on a spiritual level, has an affinity with the Heart chakra. It harmonises relationships, and encourages compassion and the establishment of strong bonds.

★ Emerald is reputedly a stone of constancy in love, and is said to have been brought to Earth from the planet Venus. Because it is green, it also holds deep associations with the Heart chakra.

★ Rhodochrosite can be used to attract one's soul mate. This stone, as with all the pink stones, can be used as an effective love magnet. It encourages you to appreciate yourself by teaching you that you are worthy of love, wholeness and happiness - and so opening you up to receive.

★ Malachite, Citrine, Rhodonite, Moonstone, Morganite, Beryl, Ruby, Mangano Calcite, Garnet, Red and Pink Tourmaline, Tugtupite, Rutilated Quartz, Lodestone, Peridot and Lapis Lazuli are also known for their love properties, and can be used or worn to invite romance into your life, or to bring and retain enduring love.

★ Clear Quartz can be used with any of these listed crystals to amplify their metaphysical properties.

★ Shells: Although shells are not technically a crystal, but rather a natural elemental material, they are associated with love and are sacred to Aphrodite, the Greek love goddess, and are often used in magic talismans to attract romance.

★ ESSENTIAL OILS ★

The following essential oils are known for their aphrodisiac or love-attracting properties also, and can be worn as perfumes on the skin, used in an oil burner or vaporiser, dispersed in a bath, used in spell-casting and wishing rituals, sprinkled on your pillow to imbue your dreams with inspired romantic notions, or in any other creative ways you can think of! **

★ Essential oils, flowers and herbs which contain natural pheromones or like substances, or increase pheromone levels in the body, are: Lavender, Frankincense, Jasmine, Nutmeg, Ylang Ylang, Sandalwood, Patchouli and Asian Agarwood (Oud).

★ The prime love oil, which holds Universal appeal, is rose. Reputedly excellent for both the mind and body, roses are the basis of more than 95 per cent of women's fragrances, and the petals have a long tradition of uplifting the spirits and soothing the soul. *Rosa damascena* is believed to be good for attracting love, while *R. centifolia*, the French rose oil base, is regarded as an aphrodisiac. Rose is traditionally accepted as the all-encompassing Universal fragrance of love, blessed with a reputation for opening up the hearts of all those who come under its spell.

★ Cedarwood oil has been used since ancient times in incense and perfumes. Its deep, woody scent helps to stimulate the Base chakra, increasing sexual passion and desire. Its sedative qualities aid relaxation and encourage openness. In herbal magic, it is also associated with spells for wealth and abundance.

★ Neroli, Geranium, Almond (as a base), Basil, Thyme, Vetiver, Gardenia, Vanilla, Rose Otto, Apple, Cardamom, Lotus, Orange, Ginger, Bergamot, Rosewood and Clary Sage are also exquisitely seductive and sensual, and can be used in any way you like to bring to you that which your heart desires. These oils, when mixed with your own pheromones and magical intentions, will naturally enhance your point of attraction!

** Always research first and use with caution.

LEO ★ LOVE STYLE

Love makes the world go round for the big-hearted, bold, spectacular Lion. Profoundly romantic and generous with your affection, one of your main ways of demonstrating your love is to lavish gifts on your partner. If your gifts are received well and appreciated, you will be chuffed, if not, you will feel put out. Above all, you need attention, praise, adoration and respect from your lovers - and indeed, *everyone*. You are extremely loyal and faithful and once committed you play the role of grand lover perfectly. Anyone who does not give this tends to put your Fire out, if it ever took hold in the first place. Detached, aloof, distant and hard-to-get prospects are not your style. To Leo, love is a creative act, and something which must be constantly shown and shared with each other through the exchange of gestures, play, cuddles and of course sex: Leo is, after Scorpio, possibly the most amorous sign of the zodiac. Leo is a supportive and encouraging, if not a little bossy and possessive, lover. You like to play hard, love hard and work hard, so your friends and lovers must fit into your hectic schedule. When you allow others to make some of the plans and run the show at least some of the time, your romantic ride will be smoother and easier. Your spontaneity, affectionate, loyal and romantic nature will attract many admirers. Showy and ardent, you are a stylish partner whose attitude to love is one of great artistry and skill. Deeply protective and proud of your partner, you will defend them loyally and protectively. But in return, you not only expect loyalty and fidelity of your beloved, you demand to be treated like a King or Queen yourself. And once you have found that special someone who can give and take all of the above, you are both in for an exciting magical carpet ride of exquisite fun, big love and grand adventure.

LUCKY IN LOVE?
LEO COMPATIBILITY

* Please note the following is based on your Sun sign alone. For a whole and integrated approach to relationship compatibility, your whole natal chart would need to be taken into consideration. Synastry (*syn*: acting or considered together, united; *astry*: pertaining to the stars) is a branch of astrology which delves into more complex areas, and is based upon the natal charts of the two people concerned, to determine overall compatibility, potential conflicts and suitability based upon celestial influences. For the purposes of length, the below information is simplified and only refers to Sun sign connections.

Leo ★ Aries ♌ ♈

Double the dose of vitality and energy plus makes you two a dynamic duo! Fun, games, and ego-trips galore will reign supreme here. Fire and Fire work well together and you find Leo entertaining, while Leo enjoys the Arien energy. Aries must beware of wounding the Leonine pride with his blunt frankness however, as this is no mere pussycat he is dealing with here. Both being Fire signs, you share bossiness, enthusiasm, courage, vibrancy, boldness and an insatiable desire for attention, praise and ego-stroking; in the case of the latter, one of you may have to move over to let the other one shine occasionally, otherwise there is a very real danger of ego clashes and the resultant tantrums. Your finer Fire qualities can be used constructively to form a wonderful bond between you, but there will inevitably be battles of wills, especially if the Ram hurts the Leo's fragile pride, in which case he will either lash out at the Aries with all paws blazing (after which he will forgive and promptly forget), or slink off somewhere to lick his wounds. Usually, he will be back for another round, as the Lion is intensely loyal and needs the support of his special other. This team has good overall prospects for happiness and fulfilment in love. You are both temperamental, warm, dramatic, vain and emotionally open - Aries just need to work on refining his flattery skills and letting his own self fall away from time to time, and the Lion will surely reward the Ram with his faithfulness and wholehearted affections. Overall, if used positively, Leo and Aries can share a joyful and stimulating relationship. And if you can make room for the two of you in the partnership, it will burn even bigger and brighter.

Overall compatibility rating ★ 8 out of 10.
Lucky Romance Tip ★ To attract an Aries, wear the colours red or orange, and use the crystal diamond.

Leo ★ Taurus ♌ ♉

The sleepy Bull challenges the Lion's need for drama and excitement, and Leo may find it difficult when Taurus tries to possess him or shows little enthusiasm for his grandiose plans or ideals. Although both Fixed types, you both express this quality in different ways. If Taurus enjoys and praises Leo's posturing while gently holding her own ground, she might find a whole new world. You are both extravagant, with a love of luxury, good quality things, and material pleasures, which is a mutual and advantageous aspect to your relationship. But Earth with Fire in two such strong-willed signs can cause conflict and opposition unless you both learn to compromise and practice some give and take. Leo thrives on the attention, affection and adoration which Taurus so readily and naturally gives to her special loved one, while Taurus appreciates Leo's fine taste, chivalry, big heart, demonstrative nature and unrivalled sense of style. Usually the Bull is quite content to be dominated by her Lion, but if she tolerates it for too long without saying anything, she can charge like her namesake! Leo's big, often grandiose ideas can be unsettling for the conservative Taurus, and Taurus's inflexibility and dull nature may grate on the buoyant, dynamic Leo's nerves. If you can capitalise on your mutual love of indulgent pleasures such as good food, wine, art, leisure and theatre, this relationship stands a good, solid chance of surviving - after all, the Fixed signs are known for their endurance and stoic perseverance, and this could prove a fine example.

Overall compatibility rating ★ 7 out of 10.
Lucky Romance Tip ★ To attract a Taurus, wear the colours pink or green, and use the crystal rose quartz.

Leo ★ Gemini ♌ ♊

You both love to play and joke, so you can have some great fun together. But although Leo is stimulated and intrigued by the tricky, cunning Gemini's cheekiness, he doesn't quite trust it. Leo represents dignity, while Gemini is imprudent. The Twins may find Leo too pompous, and the Lion may see the Twins as frivolous. If you can overcome this mutual disapproval, you may have a stimulating, enlightening relationship. Overall, Fire and Air are a compatible combination. Gemini fans Leo's flames with his wit and charm, but the Lion's delicate pride will be hurt and he will stride away if the Gemini flirts with other people. As Air and Fire blend well together, a healthy, fun-loving rapport can be easily built up between you, which is always a good starting point and foundation for any relationship. Leo's broad vision and warm nature will appeal to Gemini, but the Lion's desire to be boss and take control of the relationship can sometimes unsettle Gemini's free spirit. These qualities can be used constructively to form a wonderful bond between you, but there will inevitably be clashes of wills, especially if the Gemini takes flight, as he is prone to do on a frequent basis, and the Lion doesn't get his way. Leo needs adoration, praise and to be the centre of attention, and will not always appreciate Gemini's need for sharing and social stimulation with so many others. Leo's pride can be easily wounded by Gemini's independence and lack of consistent affection. Overall, if used positively, the Lion and the Twins can share a joyful and stimulating relationship, if they can overcome their differences. Indeed, Air will usually fuel the Fire here, making it burn bigger and brighter. And if each partner is happy to allow the other to do his/her own thing, this has the potential to be a sparkling union of dazzling proportions.

Overall compatibility rating ★ 8 out of 10
Lucky Romance Tip ★ To attract a Gemini, wear the colours light blue or yellow, and use the crystal citrine

Leo ★ Cancer * ♌ ♋

As the 'father' and 'mother' of the zodiac, your Fire and Water combination has the potential to be a good one. However, Cancer may be a little clingy and needy for the more extroverted Lion's spirit. But although Cancer's Water is not compatible with Leo's Fire, your rulers the Moon and the Sun *do* complement each other, so despite your very different natures there is a chance here for a strong bond. The Crab will often have to give way to the dominant Lion, but the latter has the qualities which make Cancer's Moon shine brighter. Moreover, Leo needs the adoration, attention and praise which the Cancerian is more than happy to give, and Cancer will certainly never wish to take the shine off Leo's limelight. Leo can create drama, and Cancer will patiently nurture her Lion through these outbursts. But Cancer will have to impose limits on how much energy she gives to the Leo's persistent need for theatrics, as it can be draining to the Crab's sensitive psyche. Also, the Lion is known to roar, rant, rave and boldly state his opinion, which could trample the Cancerian's delicate feelings and leave her feeling hurt. However sensitive Cancer is, she always knows exactly what she wants and the Leo will admire her for this - as long as she doesn't outshine him. He will also adore the Cancerian's cooking and knack of keeping house, for he loves beauty, comfort and a secure environment almost as much as she does. In any case, these two will likely take turns in playing the emotional dramatist in the relationship, but they have vastly different styles of expressing their innermost feelings: The Lion will roar, while the Crab will sulk. Leo likes to bear responsibility, and Cancer will appreciate his chivalry, generosity, affection and warmth. Around the Cancerian, the Lion may very well dull his roar to a loud, contented purr - after all, he is a soft fluffy kitten at heart, and Cancer will bring out his best in this regard. If Cancer's over-sentimentality and emphasis on emotions doesn't weigh the relationship down too strongly, these two could make much fun - and an epic love story - together, because, as this duo demonstrates, Water sometimes makes the Fire positively sizzle!

Overall compatibility rating ★ 5 out of 10.
Lucky Romance Tip ★ To attract a Cancerian, wear the colours silver or white, and use the crystal moonstone.

Leo ★ Leo ♌ ♌

Lions in love really romp and roar. This is no quiet romance, and your passion, big plans, sharing of fun, and stimulating power struggles will ensure there is never a dull moment between you. However, every Lion and Lioness needs to be the centre of attention, so the two of you together could be a little too tempestuous and competitive for long-term prospects. Fire and Fire in two such positive, strong-willed people can prove to be either an epic love story or a giant failure. Mutual give and take will be necessary if this partnership is to work. But you do understand each other's need for the limelight and if you can manage to share the stage at the same time in unison, this could be a wonderful adventure and larger than life romance. There may be massive tantrums and tempers may flare, but after you have both stormed backstage to lick your wounds, you are usually happy to come back for another act. You are both affectionate, loving, loyal and magnetic, qualities which take the edge of your bossy and overbearing ways. And moreover, with your combined ambition, enthusiasm and organisational skills, you could achieve lofty goals if you can manage to share the Sun that beams down brightly - if not, you may just burn each other out completely. Since compromising is not exactly Leo's forte, figuring out who will hold the sceptre, as well as the hierarchical order of the relationship, can become your greatest challenge. But if you can overcome the crown fights, your relationship can become a raging bonfire!

Overall compatibility rating ★ 7 out of 10
Lucky Romance Tip ★ To attract a Leo, wear the colours gold or orange, and use the crystal ruby

Leo ★ Virgo ♌ ♍

The Lion is often unprepared for the Virgin's fastidious tastes, and Virgo will find Leo too demanding of praise. The Virgin does however appreciate the way these big pussycats will have a go at anything; their bravery and bigness of heart inspires and uplifts the modest and reserved Virgo. The Virgin both frustrates and fascinates Leo. This has the potential to be a love-hate situation, as the Virgo's incessant criticism can wound the Lion's delicate ego. Cool and hot temperaments don't always blend well either. A certain degree of tolerance is called for here, and the Virgin is happy to let the Lion have his time in the Sun without interfering, for she is more than happy to work away in the background. There may not be a big enough degree of intimacy for the sparks to really fly, but if you can respect each other's differences, this has a fair chance of being a sensual, albeit understated union. Virgo's introversion may grate the more extroverted, expressive Leo, and Leo's extravagance and large appetite for life may unsettle the calm, cool and collected Virgo. Leo may also become annoyed by Virgo's obsession with detail and emotional restraint, and her nit-picking and criticism may well hurt the Lion's fragile pride. The playful Lion needs love, fun and adventure, while the Virgo needs peace, orderliness and efficient, no-nonsense consistency - the Lion's theatrics and flair for drama will unravel her already frayed nerves. Earthy Virgo is moderate and retiring, while Fiery Leo is dominant and likes to be in control, so the success of this union may be questionable. Leo's ardent emotions will sometimes overwhelm the self-contained Virgo, which could prove their breaking point. The Lion is a social animal who adores praise, the Virgin is a quiet, steady achiever who revels in solitude. This may or may not sit too well with the Lion, who has a big heart that he loves to share, and he enjoys the thrill of grand romances and demonstrative displays of affection and adoration, which the Virgin is unlikely to provide. That extra spark for passion may well prove elusive between these two.

Overall compatibility rating ★ 5.5 out of 10
Lucky Romance Tip ★ To attract a Virgo, wear the colours white or yellow, and use the crystal sapphire

Leo ★ Libra ♌ ♎

The roaring Lion can be hugely attractive to the impressionable Libran, yet if the Fire dwindles your relationship rapidly wears thin. Libra's fence-sitting may irritate the more decisive, determined Leo.
Libra's charm and grace soothes the Lion's Fiery soul, yet the Scales' indefinite, fluctuating rhythms can frustrate Leo's need for action, drama and excitement. But Fire is compatible with Air and since both of you have the natural ability for enjoying all the good things in life, there is no doubt many happy times will be had together. In any case, you are both charming, sociable, friendly and loving. Libra has an ethereal, measured approach to those good things in life however, and the Lion's extravagance, lavishness, generosity and flamboyance may well upset the

Libran's fine need for balance and peace. Despite this, the Lion will be most impressed by the Libran's impeccable manners, style and good (and expensive) tastes, and the Scales will appreciate the Leo's chivalry, warmth and even vanity. A curious feature in your partnership is that although Leo likes to be boss, Libra is an efficiently cool customer and will be able to tactfully and artfully manipulate the Lion - and the Lion will never know it. Libra is much more diplomatic than Leo, who likes to get his own way, but this difference does not necessarily make for a clash of wills. Overall, you are likely to get along just fine and make a successful and happy partnership through developing a fun-loving, light-hearted rapport. The Lion just needs to tone down his loud roar to suit the Libran's innate need for balance and harmony, and romantic bliss can indeed be yours.

Overall compatibility rating ★ 8.5 out of 10
Lucky Romance Tip ★ To attract a Libran, wear the colours pink and blue, and use the crystal opal

Leo ★ Scorpio * ♌ ♏

When the Lion roars and the Scorpion is poised and ready to sting, you know this may be a challenging match. Yet Scorpio's sincere compliments and smouldering passion bring out Leo's enthusiasm, invoke his loyalty and stoke his Fire. But different in nature with the exception of your Fixed mode, you two are usually at odds with each other. Scorpio's internal feelings and your external actions can easily clash. In addition, the Scorpion's jealousy, intensity and possessiveness can seem all too difficult for the Lion, who does not like to be controlled or bossed around. Frank, extroverted Leo will rarely understand or appreciate Scorpio's secretive, hidden motives and manipulative manoeuvres and cool, defensive character. Scorpio guards her secrets, while heart-on-sleeve Leo lays everything on the table. Further, the what-you-see-is-what-you-get Lion may not understand the Scorpio's complex and deeply emotional nature, and Scorpio will in turn find it difficult to trust Leo with her innermost feelings. But there does exist a strong sexual magnetism between you and this could make for a very passionate, physical relationship. Long-term success will depend on whether or not your egos clash and whether you can practise give and take without one trying to dominate the other. The fact that you are both uncompromising may work for or against you. You are both powerful and magnetic, so if you really put your strong wills and ambitious minds together, great heights are very possible.

Overall compatibility rating ★ 6.5 out of 10
Lucky Romance Tip ★ To attract a Scorpio, wear the colours red or burgundy, and use the crystal malachite

Leo ★ Sagittarius ♌ ♐

You two Fire signs have a natural empathy and an easy harmony. However, the competitive sparks between you can engulf you and leave both your prides and egos battered in the rubble of embers.

However, two Fire signs can also spark wonderful discussions and mind games. You stimulate and understand each other, yet the Archer's restless spirit and elusive ways may leave the Lion cold. Independent Sagittarius may rebel if Leo tries to boss or control him, and the Lion's fragile pride might feel starved or neglected if Sagittarius is too eager for freedom and wider horizons. The Archer has little time for tantrums and theatrics, and the Lion finds the Archer's blunt indifference to romance a bit off-putting. Non-committal Sagittarius may upset the Leo's need for a more consistent brand of love, with the Archer's free spirit winning out over being tied down to anything or anyone. Still, Leo is impressed by the confident, active, self-confident and enthusiastic Sagittarian, and both of you enjoy extravagance, discussion and drama. You share a love of the social circuit, both being warm, friendly, open and welcoming to all and sundry, and unlike any other zodiacal matches, it doesn't seem to matter to the Lion if the Archer doesn't worship him. An outgoing and lively relationship, your rulers the Sun and Jupiter, exert a powerfully positive and optimistic influence over your union. Both generous and open-hearted, you will more than likely enrich each other and on the whole your similarities will override your differences. Overall, the Lion and the Centaur are both powerful beasts, so your animal passions could be stirred enough to evoke some pretty amazing sparks here.

Overall compatibility rating ★ 9 out of 10

Lucky Romance Tip ★ To attract a Sagittarius, wear the colour deep purple or royal blue, and use the crystal zircon

Leo ★ Capricorn ♌ ♑

The Lion's need for praise and centre stage irritates and confuses the modest Goat, and since you two are at odds by nature and differ in almost every respect, this romance has the potential to be a huge learning experience. Capricorn's Earth can put out Leo's Fire, particularly in this case. Although you are both strong, determined personalities, you are very different; the Lion needs fun and action, while the Goat needs calm, steady progress. As well, Leo enjoys the journey while Capricorn revels in the destination. Capricorn will seem distant and aloof to the open and friendly Leo and her lack of spontaneity may be frustrating to the demonstrative and playful Lion. The Goat's cool, indifferent nature may hurt Leo's precious pride and is at odds with the Lion's warm, outgoing expression. Your rulers the Sun and Saturn, also differ considerably - the brilliant, grandiose Sun seeks to shine and experience, while the austere, conservative Saturn strives for practical and serious applications. Frugal, sensible Capricorn will not tolerate Leo's extravagant, lavish, generous lifestyle, and joyful and affectionate Leo will find Capricorn's veiled sensuality too difficult to reach. Leo likes to live life to the full, in the here and now, whereas Capricorn, being more cautious, needs to plan for the future. Capricorn will show calm reserve if Leo sulks, and the Lion will seek more amorous company if he feels that Capricorn doesn't care. However, Leo has the power to melt the Goat's ice and if Capricorn can let her guard down, she is caring, giving and devoted, providing a stable, nurturing and steadying influence to the relationship. Further, she is disciplined enough to recognise when and where the partnership may need work, and will dedicate all her energies and resources into making it work if she feels it is worthwhile. If the Goat can lighten up a little and the Lion can learn to live with Capricorn's seriousness, these two have a reasonably good chance of bridging the gap between them. In any case, they will be unfailingly loyal to one another if the relationship is worth their effort.

Overall compatibility rating ★ 6 out of 10
Lucky Romance Tip ★ To attract a Capricorn, wear the colours brown or black, and use the crystal garnet

Leo ★ Aquarius ♌ ♒

While you are astrological opposites, you are not necessarily psychological opposites, as your elements, Air and Fire, blend well together. In fact, being cosmic opposites, they have much to teach each other, and each can learn invaluable relationship lessons from the other. Both being Fixed signs, you also share strong minds, fixed opinions, a strong determination and each a mind of your own. These qualities can be used constructively to form a wonderful bond between you, but there will inevitably be clashes of wills, especially if the Water

Bearer takes flight, as they are prone to do from time to time, and the Lion doesn't get his way. The Lion appreciates the Water Bearer's quirky sense of humour, but the Aquarian's cool demeanour can dampen this romance somewhat. Leo will not understand why Aquarius should be so unpredictable, detached and unreachable at the most unexpected times and for no apparent reason. Leo needs adoration, praise and to be the centre of attention, and will not always appreciate Aquarius's need for sharing and caring on a wider scale. Leo's pride can be easily wounded by Aquarius's independence and lack of consistent affection, and although you both enjoy varied company, the Water Bearer is more detached and impersonal in social groups. Overall, if used positively, Leo and Aquarius can share a joyful and stimulating relationship, if they can overcome their differences. Indeed, Air will usually fuel the Fire here, making it burn bigger and brighter.

Overall compatibility rating ★ 7.5 out of 10
Lucky Romance Tip ★ To attract an Aquarian, wear the colours electric blue or turquoise, and use the crystal aquamarine

Leo ★ Pisces * ♌ ♓

You two have the potential to make a charming and romantic pair, but this is either a creative combination or a quagmire! The mushy Piscean emotions can either bog the Lion down or inspire his best efforts. Your ruling planets, Neptune and the Sun, exercise two very different energies in the relationship; the Sun may indeed outshine the more retiring, timid Neptune. Further, your elements, Water and Fire, and your modes, Mutable and Fixed, don't blend easily. Pisces has deep, mysterious and elusive qualities, which are unfathomable to most people, including the big-hearted, open Leo. While Pisces admires the strength and purpose of Leo, you both live in different worlds and may fail to really 'see' each other - Pisces, due to having rose-coloured glasses on, and Leo, due to wanting to be centre stage and being blinded by the spotlight. The Fish will sometimes prove too emotional and 'out-there' for the 'here-and-now', frank Leonian extrovert. The Leo needs recognition, admiration and praise, which the Pisces is only too happy to give, but the Fish can be so often residing in the clouds, that Leo may have trouble bringing her back down to Earth for long enough to watch his performance. Both are romantic, emotionally expressive and a little dramatic, but express these in entirely different ways, although both being big-hearted, are equally as capable of bringing out the best in the other, and as such, this can be an exquisitely inspiring match. The Leo thrives on ego and pride, and may hurt the much gentler, quieter Fish's sensitive feelings by being too direct, bossy or dominating. The Fish will rarely have her spot in the Sun with the Lion around, and may swim off in the other direction if her needs aren't being fulfilled. Nonetheless, with a love of receiving flattery and just as big a love for giving it, Leo will court Pisces with all the grandeur and romance of a Knight in Shining Armour if he feels the catch is worth casting his line for - and Pisces will more than likely be reeled in and swept off her feet by her bold King.

Overall compatibility rating ★ 6.5 out of 10
Lucky Romance Tip ★ To attract a Pisces, wear the colours mauve or sea green, and use the crystal amethyst

* With all Fire and Water combinations (i.e. Leo with Cancer, Scorpio or Pisces), it is easy to see how and why fire and water are natural enemies. Water can quickly put a fire out, and fire can dry up water. Fire usually works quickly, and water gently. In alchemy and astrology, both are important, and both must be carefully manipulated and controlled to make full effective use of their powerful, albeit vastly differing, natures. Fire can be brought back to a steady heat, whereas the pressure and force of water can be increased vigorously or to circulate more actively. As warm and watery beings, the human body demonstrates the miracle of fire and water combined. Water connects, flows and lubricates, and brings healing, its passive, gentle nature soothing away the scorching harshness of fire. One ancient text offers a mystical view of how water and fire are intertwined in the body, and suggests that it is through consciously combining these two elements that we can transform our inner state. Fire can initiate and inspire this quest for self-transformation, but once the fire burns down, life can be restored anew by water. Natural enemies? Mostly. Astrological passion? Absolutely!

YOUR TAROT CARDS ★ FOR LUCK, MAGIC, ENERGY, ABUNDANCE, QUESTING & MEANING
STRENGTH, THE SUN & JUDGEMENT

Tarot and astrology are inextricably linked. All the cards of the Major Arcana, which comprises 22 of the Tarot's 78 cards, are 'ruled by' or connected with either one of the twelve zodiac signs, the planets and luminaries, or one of the four elements.

The 22 Major Arcana cards contain the richest symbolism of all the cards in the Tarot deck, each carrying a myriad of messages for the reader to decipher. The symbolism contained within these images represents the archetypal aspects of your character. It also describes the path your soul takes through each stage of life, revealing clues through which you can explore different parts of yourself. Each of the cards also represents an aspect of Universal human experience and has a name that either directly conveys the meaning of the card, such as Strength or Justice, or depicts individuals that represent these human archetypes, such as the Hermit or the Empress. The illustrations on each card contain one or more figures and tuning into a card's imagery enables you to grasp its meaning intuitively. Consider the demeanour of the characters, whether it is day or night, the background, any symbols, the buildings, the colours, the vegetation, the weather and the season. Every card has its own story to impart, and through entering that story you can gain deeper insights into the full picture of your journey so far, as well as illuminating your path ahead.

I have outlined three cards here for your sign: Strength, The Sun and Judgement, which all have links to your zodiac sign itself Leo, your ruler the Sun, and your element of Fire. All three cards will have special meaning for your sign, and can carry powerful messages and lessons for you to reflect upon.

★ STRENGTH ★
Ruled by Leo

Keywords ★ Force, Courage, Power

★ KEY THEMES ★
Courage ★ Fortitude ★ Moral Fibre ★ Firmness ★ Power ★ Confidence ★ Great Inner Strength ★ Forgiveness ★ Compassion ★ Patience ★ Willpower ★ The Courage of Your Convictions ★ Belief in own Strength ★ Gentle Force ★ Determination ★ Domination of Instincts ★ Tranquil Strength ★ Dauntlessness ★ Triumph ★ Control of a Situation ★ Victory Achieved Through a Gentle, Measured Approach

Number ★ 8 (or 11 in some decks)
Astrological Sign ★ Leo

THE MESSAGE ★ Sometimes called Fortitude, this is one of the three virtues that appear in the Tarot deck - the others are Justice and Temperance. The Strength card will appear when you need to know that you're stronger than you realise and that you can definitely handle your current challenges. However, instead of using force and barging through obstacles, you're better off with an approach of compassion, gentleness and firm kindness, as the strength that your setbacks call for can only come from the softness of a harmonious spiritual core. You need to release harsh judgements and practice forgiveness and patience, and your strength and effectiveness will increase. You need to believe in yourself and your ability to grow from your trials. Strength can alternatively mean that you are experiencing yourself as ready and able to get what you want in life. Grounded and centred in your experience of energy, you know from the *heart* what you need.

THE STORY ★ Strength is a situation which is well in-hand, controlled, and of which one is in charge. It signifies a courageous person, endowed with a tranquil strength, a resolute temperament and sound self-control. The lady depicted in most decks has tamed the animal's wild nature with her spiritual touch. She has no need of physical strength, for by love she has conquered. The crown the lion wears in common symbolism signifies that he is King of the Beasts, while the brave young woman on the Strength Tarot card, with the sign for 'infinity' crowning her highest energy centre, renders her the Queen of Strength. By conquering the natural fears of her own bestial nature she has harnessed the infinite power of her spirit.

THE AWAKENING ★ In the face of fear, act calmly and with love and you will gain the true strength of an integrated body and spirit. Through gentleness you will accomplish what force cannot. Strength promises victory to those who know how to direct their natural gifts and willpower into the right channels, and who persevere in their efforts with unflagging energy and focus. It is through the power of inner peace and love that the character featured on this card is able to tame the fearsome beast and can open his mouth with sheer will but little physical effort. Indeed, the strength of her soul and the force of her love will tame the lion more effectively than any violence, aggression or savagery. She represents the overcoming of difficulties and weaknesses of character through steady persistence. The lion symbolises power and positive energy, and the human figure harnesses that power. Drawing this card will always make you the master of yourself and/or the situation in which you find yourself. It tells you that, if you handle circumstances in a positive, concentrated and gentle manner, you will achieve your aim.

THE LESSON ★ Strength indicates that personal courage and discipline are required in order to reach a goal. The struggle between human and lion is a reflection of bravery, and although the portrayal of a person fighting this beast is depicted as a physical one, it also relates to inner struggles. The message is to keep going through a difficult situation instead of running away from it. This does not suggest that you should put up with being bullied, but on the contrary, quietly and courageously stand up to tyranny. Truth, light, tact and diplomacy are far more effective, and will win you respect and admiration.

SYMBOLISM *★ Strength's symbolism lies in the reconciling of your base instincts, the taming of your wild instincts and primal desires, with your higher levels of will and consciousness. Its message is in keeping with the evolutionary process of the Self depicted in the Major Arcana: the development of self-knowledge that raises your awareness to a high understanding and fuller integration of your whole self. It represents passion for life that provides the energy to overcome even tough challenges. A symbol of the ultimate the life force expression, Strength gives you the knowing that you are grounded and strong, stronger indeed than you think.

The Strength card features a powerful human figure (the conscious mind), sometimes male and sometimes female, fighting to prise open the jaws of a lion (the untamed instincts), conquering the beast without the use of his club (or force). The club, which is lying on the ground, is apparently redundant, revealing that physical weapons are not necessary when the force of pure will is available and utilised.

The lion struggles against the person, but has evidently already accepted his defeat. This symbolises the conscious mind having supremacy over the primal animal nature.

As this card is ruled by Leo, it also signifies honour, reliability, honesty and a fixed sense of purpose. The gentle firmness depicted in its imagery is representative of the higher, immortal spiritual self, which means this card is telling us not to allow our rational, objective mind (the lion) to overrule our spiritual wisdom (the woman). The brim of the lady's hat is in the shape of a figure of eight, the symbol of infinity, which is also worn by the Magician, further emphasising her connection with inner wisdom and the ethereal realms

Divinatory meanings of the Strength card are firstly strength, and also courage, power, conviction, resolution, energy, defiance, action, confidence, zeal, mind over matter or matter over mind, and accomplishment. It symbolises resolute action and a willingness to boldly stand up for what is right, regardless of the consequences. Other themes are physical strength, a fight for fair play, courage in defeating mean attitudes and hatred, and rapid health improvement if illness has been recently experienced. Furthermore, you will triumph over enemies and setbacks.

When working with this card, ask yourself how you can strengthen your own sense of purpose to succeed on your journey, and remember that progress on the path to self-discovery is made through gentle strength, not severity. Its message is that there is no need to worry or lose sight of your goals, for even though the road you are on may seem difficult, you will get there in the end. Patience, perseverance and self-awareness are needed to keep you on track. You also need to nurture your spirit, fortify your morals and foster self-discipline.

This card is a good indication of recovery from illness or other difficulties and may describe a situation that must be confronted bravely even though you are fearful. The Strength card represents the power of healing by the bringing forth of the 'feminine force', into a place where wild animals are tamed and the world of unseen forces is explored through it.

Overall, the image in Strength signifies that if the inner animal urges within each of us can be used positively and without overuse of force, great things can be achieved and any adversities can be easily overcome through the use of your vast inner resources.

Leos are recommended to carry one of these cards with them to illumine their paths, and to magnetise that for which they are asking. Go forth and claim the magic which is yours by using the symbolism of Strength as your guide!

★ THE SUN ★
Ruled by the Sun

Keywords ★ Success, Joy, Vitality

★ KEY THEMES ★
★ Optimism ★ Joy ★ Positive Energy ★ Merriment ★ Exuberance ★ Clarity ★ Positive Outlook ★ Freedom ★ Blossoming ★ Public Recognition ★ Great Personal Insights ★ Vibrant Health ★ Fulfilment ★ Play ★ Success ★ Abundance ★ Enlightenment ★ Pure Feelings ★ Perfect Happiness ★ Radiance ★ Rejoicing ★ Satisfaction ★ Delight ★ Charisma ★ Magnetism ★ Affinities ★ Union ★ Profound and Complete Joy ★

Number ★ 19
Astrological Sign ★ Leo

THE STORY ★ Two almost naked children, perhaps the celestial Castor and Pollux, the Gemini of the zodiac, are standing in front of a wall with the Sun above casting down radiant rays, falling like drops of gold around them. Some decks show a beaming Sun gazes down on a naked child riding a white horse. The child holds up a banner, and behind him is a wall, over which sunflowers, the ultimate symbol of the Sun, can be seen. Whichever child or children the card shows, the Sun symbolises the Divine, wise child, who reminds you how to play. In idyllic scenes from childhood, everything is open and always flooded with the Sun's rays. This card allows you to freely open your heart to the world. There are no boundaries and no secrets. The Sun in the card casts strong rays of light on a loving couple, or children, who represent love, friendship and rapport. They are protected from outside evil influences by a sturdy, well-built but quite low wall. However, we get the impression that the characters are becoming overheated by the Sun's powerful energy, serving as a reminder that although the Sun is a cheering presence, it can also burn you; you must beware of over-exertion as it can lead to burn-out.

THE AWAKENING ★ Everything will be sunny and bright. Love, relationships and friendships of all kinds will be highlighted. This is a time to emulate the Sun's active, creative ability to realise new works of art or love, and to be a dynamic, inspiring and influential leader whose lights shines for all to see and be warmed by. The Sun is a very lucky omen, and perhaps the happiest, most positive card in the Tarot. The introspection you have experienced enables you to better understand yourself and opens you to a well of pure joy that bubbles up and overflows throughout all areas of your life. You are brimming with love for the world, your energy is increased and you can now focus on realising your dreams. Success abounds!

THE LESSON ★ Quite simply, the Sun urges you to give in to satisfaction, contentment, spontaneous and pure feelings, and to be yourself. The presence of the Sun is a good omen, a sign of relief, clarity, success and abundance. It suggests that you should also encourage others to enjoy life. If you are thinking of starting or increasing your family, the Sun gives you this blessing. It also tells you that all that is true, good, just and beautiful will triumph.

SYMBOLISM ★★ Just as the Moon is the deeper female aspect, the Sun is the overt masculine principle, the creative element that impregnates the female to bring forth life. Without the union of male and female there is only sterility and stagnation. Having received a glimpse of the female archetype in the Moon, the Tarot traveller is now shown the male archetype of the Sun.

The Sun card symbolises happiness, growth, the light of knowledge, freedom, wonder, blossoming, life-affirming energy, joy, playfulness, creativity and pure love.

The Sun in the card shines upon the young couple and landscape below, yet its brightness is directed indiscriminately, which shows that its light is available for the use of everyone. It represents the knowledge that we are all connected by the eternal rays of the life force, that life is a joyous circus and everyone is in the ring together. The Sun card employs generous imagery - the sunshine illuminates all that it falls upon, and spreads it far and wide.

Some cards may include a butterfly, which is the archetypal symbol of rebirth and metamorphosis. Through learning of its process of moving out of a chrysalis state and into the light, transformed, we can experience the miracle of the butterfly - emerging from our cocoons, we unfurl our wings, and soar into the Sun-soaked heavens, utterly changed.

In other cards a huge, brilliant Sun hangs over the Earth, dropping beads of sparkling dew, brightening and ripening everything - and everyone - beneath it. In other decks, The Sun frequently shows a naked child riding a white horse. The child is a sign of new life and hope. Behind him is a wall, over which sunflowers are seen, or the sunflowers may be shown on open ground. In some decks the child actually holds the Sun, while in others a massive Sun dominates the sky. Oranges and sunflowers, both Solar images, often adorn the scene. Sunflowers can be said to symbolise the four elements of Earth, Air, Fire and Water.

Overall, the mood and symbolism of this card is buoyant and happy. The glorious Sun bestows the gift of life to all the Universe. The child, without saddle or bridle, represents the perfect control between the conscious and unconscious mind. The child's nakedness shows that he has nothing to hide.

The Sun is the nineteenth card of the Major Arcana, and heralds a time of joy and progress. While The Moon signifies uncertainty and doubt, The Sun symbolises clear vision, a positive attitude and confidence. The Sun is a symbol of masculine energy, and its divinatory meanings are success, satisfaction, accomplishment, contentment, love, joy, favourable relationships, devotion, selfless sentiment, engagement, a happy marriage, pleasure in daily existence, warmth, high spirits, a good friend, sincerity, simple pleasures, creative achievement and liberation. Enthusiasm and joy are positive aspects connected with the Sun, but if they are not kept in check, they risk turning into negatives, in the form of insensitivity, over-confidence, extravagance, and a lack of awareness of one's limits. And although the Sun ripens the fruit, if its rays are too strong for too long, moisture can evaporate quickly and it can burn the fruit. Overall though, this is the card of success, clear skies ahead, and the promise of a sun-kissed future. Double warmth comes from its astrological link with the Sun itself, focusing on personal potential, and the dazzling light of complete self-knowledge - *magic luck*.

The Sun is obviously a daytime card and, as such, is connected with brightness, energy and clarity, unlike the dark, mysterious, shadowy night-time card of The Moon. The Sun and Moon who, in mythology, were twins, make up two halves of the whole; either one on its own would be unstable and upset the balance.

Overall, the Sun is a positive force of illumination, presaging good fortune, health, cheer and worldly success. It promotes growth and inspires vitality, energy and confidence. However, if it is too bright, it can also dazzle and blind you to the truth of a situation. It is a card indicating growth and increased potential, such as progression of relationships, financial expansion, and physical growth (as in pregnancy). The idea and understanding that Divinity is right here, in us, now - in everything and everyone - is extremely liberating.

The Sun offers you the confidence and ability to put yourself forward in the world, and allows you to radiate your personal power because you now understand your place in the Universal scheme of things, or are at least on the cusp of embracing this. This should be a creative period for you; allow your ideas to grow, flow and change, and let your true colours show. The bright yellow light radiating out of the Sun image blesses you with an enlivening sense of possibility. And above all, ask not for whom the Sun shines: because it shines for us *all*.

★ JUDGEMENT ★
Ruled by Pluto & the Element of Fire

Keywords ★ Evaluation, Opportunities, New Directions

★ KEY THEMES ★
★ Discernment ★ Karma ★ Reaping What Has Been Sown ★ Evaluation ★ Evolution ★ Review ★ Improvement ★ Revelation ★

Renewal ★ Favourable Assessment of the Facts ★ Objectivity ★ New Directions ★ Transformation ★ Legal Situations Resolved Favourably ★ Academic and Examination Success ★ Promotion ★ Bonus ★ A Career or Life Change ★ Moving in a Different Direction ★ Rehabilitation ★ Sound Decisions Based on Good Preparation and Evaluations ★ Recovery ★ Promotion ★ Admission of Guilt ★ Good News

Number ★ 20
Astrological Signs ★ Scorpio, Aries, Leo & Sagittarius

THE FOOL'S JOURNEY ★ Archetypically, Judgement means resurrection, the rebirth that comes with spiritual awareness and awakening. Arriving at this step on his journey, the Fool understands the possibilities of transformation that can come with change. The Fool reaches for enlightenment.

THE MESSAGE ★ Sometimes called the Angel, this card has a very simple but profound meaning - a second chance. Judgement portrays an end to suffering and the beginnings of a spiritual resurrection. Through Judgement, you are being offered a dissolution of negative past patterns and a resulting spiritual rebirth, the opportunity to review past events, and to offer forgiveness or make amends. Judgement symbolises a time of judgement, when souls rise from the dead to be judged. This card depicts an angel blowing a trumpet to awaken the dead from their graves, and announcing it is Judgement Day. Bodies emerge from their coffins with arms outstretched, often casting off funeral shrouds as they make ready to embrace the new life that is offered to them by the Angel of Judgement. There are usually three figures rising from the dead, to represent Mind, Body and Spirit, all of which must be brought forth to be judged. The dead are praying for mercy in the hope that the sins of their lifetimes will be forgiven. They now know that their misdemeanours are being exposed, and they are hoping to be allowed to move onto a higher plane of existence. On a spiritual wavelength, this card implies that one particular phase of your soul's journey is ending, and you will shortly assess what you learned and how you dealt with the passing situation, summing up your performance and its value to you. Judgment is telling you that at this point in your life it is time to assess and evaluate yourself, and perhaps address any underlying issues which up until now may have been ignored. To do this, you need simply to become more self-aware. Judgement emphasises that in undertaking this self-examination, you should be fair on yourself and focus on your positive character traits. It is telling you that once you have done this, like the symbolic people on the card, you will be ripe and ready to move in a new direction and onto a higher, more worthwhile plane of existence! You're either near the end of a project or at a crossroads, but either way, you are on the threshold of making an important change in your life.

THE STORY ★ The Judgement card is the respected mentor, who leads the way to a fresh perspective on life and leaves you feeling elated. Its main divinatory meanings are atonement, judgement, improvement, evaluation and finally, rebirth. In the symbolism of the Tarot, Judgement is not concerned with eternal damnation or heavenly bliss based upon this 'judgement' of your life experience so far, but instead with identifying ourselves the lessons we have learned not only from our archetypal Tarot journey so far, but through our whole life from birth onward. It is not a time for punishment and retribution, but a time of being called to account for past actions and experiences. After facing one's 'moment of truth', one can see oneself with more clarity and acceptance, and is then able to see others in the same way. This acceptance is an understanding of the human condition, human beauty, and embraces imperfections and Divine wisdom alongside each other. Our past, having been reflected upon, ensures that a positive resolution will be reinforced. With atonement and repentance, real advancement can occur. Therefore, Judgement is less about guilt and more about self-knowledge.

SYMBOLISM *★ Judgement brings you a new sense of Self. It renews and restores, and signifies that a rebirth process is taking place within the Self. A wider perspective has become available.

The angel in the card uses a trumpet, as if to call the figures from their sleepy sense of unawareness into full awakening. The cloud symbolises that this is spiritual in nature. The figures gradually rise - they are becoming released from the bonds of the past, and begin to look upwards towards an all-encompassing, broader and joyous perspective.

In some decks, the tombs are floating in a sea or river, which associates it with the notion that a river must be crossed before reaching the Promised Land. At the point of resurrection, evaluations must be made on each soul's life; therefore, this card portrays the need to reflect on life as it has been lived so far, to decide how one should proceed in the future.

This card's divinatory meanings are atonement, self-assessment, the need to repent or forgive, judgement, improvement, rebirth, rejuvenation, promotion, development, the desire for immortality, and the moment to account for the manner in which we have used our opportunities on our life's journey thus far. The Judgement card may also signify the final settlement of a matter, and a time to pay off old debts in preparation for a fresh beginning. It suggests that that which has been lying dormant will spring to life, as symbolised by the dead rising from their coffins. Judgement also indicates that the rewards for past efforts will soon finally be forthcoming.

The word 'judgement', derived from the Latin *judicem*, means 'to show or to speak what is right'. But in the context of this card, is has another meaning: discernment. As far as Judgement is concerned, discernment takes the form of distinction, recognition and separation, and all that can be accomplished. The people in the card standing beneath the figure, wearing only their nakedness, show themselves as they are, stripped of any artifice. The light within may therefore now shine forth and they no longer have any need to feel ashamed of their nudity, or to be themselves. They can discriminate between what is true or false, just or unjust. The information that has shaped their existence and made them live in hope or in fear no longer comes from external sources, but from an internal wellspring - from *themselves*. This is a revelation. For we are all assailed by outside forces which are often unconnected with our lives, that leave us feeling powerless and depressed. With such hubbub and chaos surrounding us, it is hard to hear our inner voice (depicted as the angel on this card) and see and feel the light of our own wisdom (represented by the rays of the Sun around the angel). If we cannot hear these things, how can we detect, dissect and discern? Indeed, Judgement foretells a revelation, a renewal, an inner vision that is more accurate, more profound, more objective and real. Its presence suggests that we can no longer lie to ourselves or hide the truth from others, bringing a relief, a cure, a reconciliation, a state of trust, a relaxing of tenseness, and total receptivity. It can also reveal a vocation, a promotion, a recognition or a reward that comes about as a result of our newfound inner consultations.

The Judgement card indicates that the time is ripe for a period of self-appraisal, which involves taking an honest look at yourself, your motivations and your actions. This means reviewing your accomplishments so far, neither under- or over-valuing them. It also advises that one should carefully consider how present actions affect others around them.

Ultimately, Judgement suggests that it is time to review, assess, evaluate and make some considered and thoughtful judgements regarding your life, and then make empowered decisions. To put it another way, in the words of Henry David Thoreau: "Go confidently in the direction of your dreams. Live the life you have imagined." It is time to practice discernment and then move in a new direction, from that newfound, redeemed, freed spirit.

* Please note that the images described are not found in all Tarot decks. The images in different decks can differ considerably.

THE TAROT'S SUIT OF WANDS ★ REPRESENTING THE FIRE ELEMENT

The Tarot Wands (known in some old decks as Rods, Staves or Batons) are connected with growth, creativity, enterprise, ambition, progress, initiative, work/labour, action, adventure, energy, vitality, willpower, reputation, fame, efficiency, achievement, challenge and all creative matters. The Wands represent the Fire element, and their Fire is mainly influenced by the planet Mars, which activates travel and work energy, and sexual force, but they also partake the energies of Jupiter - the Fire of benevolent warmth and expansion - and incorporate the Fire of the Sun, radiating confidence and wellbeing in all directions. Being of the Fire realm, the Wands are also associated with dynamic action, inspiration, passion and determination. Like fire itself, they signify the ignition and generation of warmth and energy, while also burning off the dross and impurities of life. Fire creates light and heat, but it can too readily burn and easily rage out of control, which can lead to destruction, ruin and havoc.

However, the energy of Fire can also be transformative. It needs fuel in order to be effective, and if this vital fuel is sourced only from the feelings, flames can be swiftly burned out. Therefore, the ultimate source of fuel for this brand of Fire lies within the self's sense of connection with the spirit - as this is a deep well that never runs dry. The narrative of the fiery Suit of Wands propels you forward and defines your actions and motivations in life. It tells of the need to create change and movement, always beginning with the initial spark that sets the flames of passion ablaze.

If Wands predominate in a reading, there's a high chance you are actively engaged in accomplishing your goals. They deal with the physical and spiritual life force - positive conflict, struggle and passion all being part of its expression. They reveal how active, dynamic, enthusiastic and passionate we are, and how these are experienced and expressed by us. There are often elements of struggle with the Wands suit, because energy needs to move freely and spontaneously, and any blockages to this have to be shifted. Conflicts within the Wands cards are generally not considered serious, and lead to a deeper, more profound sense of Self once they are resolved. They also govern inspiration and the spark that can appear out of the blue to light the way forward. In a deck of playing cards, the Wands correspond to the suit of Clubs.

THE LUCKY 13 ★ LEONINE TIPS FOR INCREASED MAGIC, LUCK & MAGNETISM

1 ★ Incorporate Leonine symbols into your daily life to remind yourself of your soul's mission.

2 ★ Use the crystal Citrine in any form in your daily life - wear it, meditate with it, hold it and carry it with you everywhere! Citrine is known in crystal healing circles as the success, prosperity, abundance and happiness stone. Citrine carries the power of your ruler the Sun, and is associated with good fortune, luck, joy and manifestation. An exceedingly beneficial stone, Citrine increases personal power and energy. A powerful cleanser and regenerator, warming, energising and highly creative, Citrine enhances all states of being and positive emotion that may assist in attracting wonderful things to you.

3 ★ Wear or surround yourself with the colours gold, orange and deep yellows.

4 ★ Learn the way of the Water Bearer by taking a humbler approach, a broader humanitarian application and a more global outlook. Aquarius has much to teach the Leonine soul. Help humankind … Put your hands in the melting pot of humanity and develop solidarity with others … Cultivate humility, modesty and tolerance … Embrace the brotherhood and sisterhood … Join a group … Let the spotlight shine on others … Cooperate … Be part of a collective movement ... Make new friends! ... Celebrate your own achievements alongside other people ... it's *all* within you!

5 ★ Use your lucky numbers 1 and 5, whenever you are needing an extra stroke of luck.

6 ★ Magnify and celebrate your self-confidence, your ability to inspire and lead others, your generosity, and your enthusiastic zest for life and drama.

7 ★ Remind yourself of your mission constantly, that is by speaking, breathing and *truly living* your dreams and insights - give them form beyond simply daydreaming about them!

8 ★ Focus your energies on exploring your uncanny flair for theatrics, and transforming yourself on life's stage in order to uplift others and make them happy. Connect with your gift for bringing out others' talents and tap into your inborn creativity through any means possible.

9 ★ Use your innate powers of leadership, organisation, authority, and childlike belief in that which is unseen, to visualise and draw that which you desire towards you. If you can develop simple faith in the positive outcome of events, you can easily use your Kingly intuition to great magnetic effect.

10 ★ Tap into and utilise your ability to make your own and others' dreams come true! But to do that, you will need to abandon your ego and self-serving interests. You may even need to step down from the stage and work behind the scenes as you learn to cultivate a humbler, albeit inherently powerful, approach.

11 ★ View your commanding/demanding nature as a strength and call forth the powers of your highly talented, gifted, unique self. Be who you *really* are, without reservation or apology, and the rest will fall into place.

12 ★ Become the 'Bright Illuminator' of others - and yourself - that you were born to be!

13 ★ Once you have mastered purer focus on others, a more Universal outlook, and a less self-serving approach to life, learn to share the resulting abundance, insights and knowledge with others so they too can walk the Higher Path!

HAVE YOU PACKED YOUR MAGICAL BAG FOR THE JOURNEY?

If you wish to increase and draw more luck, love and abundance into your life, a power pack is essential. For Leos, I would recommend carrying or wearing the following items on you on your travels. Then just sit back and watch as magic pours into your experiences and realities, both inner and outer!

★ One of each of the following gemstones: Citrine, Ruby, Peridot, Turquoise, Sardonyx
★ Tarot Cards Strength and The Sun (and the Judgement card too, if you wish)
★ A salmon in any form (use your imagination!)
★ Something made of gold
★ A heart symbol in any form
★ A postcard or image from a hot, dry place (representing your Choleric disposition). Bon Voyage!
★ A postcard from the future to yourself, proclaiming, 'Wish You Were Here!'

A FINAL WORD ★ TAPPING INTO THE MAGIC OF LEO

There is something inherently magical about Leo the Lion, the King of the zodiac jungle. Blessed with strength, courage, style, excellent taste, leadership and warmth, nothing is unnoticeable about you. The cosmos has endowed you with the precious and important gifts of ambition, loyalty, generosity, benevolence, creativity, charm and flair. Whether you are fully cognisant of it or not, a magical reservoir of energy is available to you to tap into whenever it is needed.

Inside anyone who has a strong Leo influence in their natal chart, is someone who craves to be on top of their game. You adore receiving compliments, but bless you, because you are so vulnerable to flattery that it's endearing. For you are less self-confident than you appear to be and you seek approval, love and admiration from others at any cost. Only when admired and appreciated do you truly shine, and sometimes your arrogance and boastfulness can put others off, but these are just a cover for your deeper insecurities, of which you have more than others realise. Under your courageous façade, you are in reality very sensitive, considerably tender and easily hurt, and have inner doubts about your true worth, leading to undervaluing yourself at times. Your pride and feelings are easily shaken, but you will always lick your wounds in private. But overall, you seek meaningful experiences and although you crave adoration and recognition for yourself, you are continually searching for and bringing out the best in others also. Whether you occupy a metaphorical or literal stage in the play of life, the stage is your natural home, and what better way to explore life than upon this wonderful platform?

Finally, to attune yourself to luck, harmony and success, Leonines should wear, eat, inhale, meditate upon, create, design, and dance with any or all of the suggested luck-enhancers for your Sun sign to receive the most beneficial astral vibrations these 'boosters' can offer you. Wearing, decorating and working with the amazing powers of all your lucky guides, animals, crystals, colours, woods, cards, herbs, foods, places, talismans, planetary influences, charms, numbers, and other magical tips contained within the words of this very book, will bring you greater abundance, love, magic, energy, happiness and personal power, and attract all manner of things to you like bees to sweet flowers. This, my Leonine friends, I promise you - and Aquarians *never* lie.

Good luck on the rest of your amazing life journey, and may the LUCK be with you!

Lani is also available for personal Astrology, Numerology, Aura * & Tarot reading consultations, via post, email, Skype and in-person.
Please email lalana76@bigpond.com for more information.

In-person only

Facebook Page ★ Astrology Magic

Other Books in the **Lucky Astrology** Series

Lucky Astrology ★ Aries
Lucky Astrology ★ Taurus
Lucky Astrology ★ Gemini
Lucky Astrology ★ Cancer
Lucky Astrology ★ Virgo
Lucky Astrology ★ Libra
Lucky Astrology ★ Scorpio
Lucky Astrology ★ Sagittarius
Lucky Astrology ★ Capricorn
Lucky Astrology ★ Aquarius
Lucky Astrology ★ Pisces

Order your copies now, from White Light Publishing House, at www.whitelightpublishingau.com

www.ingramcontent.com/pod-product-compliance
Lightning Source LLC
Chambersburg PA
CBHW071157300426
44113CB00009B/1231